THE
BIRDMAN
ABROAD

AN EXCLUSIVE BY STUART WINTER

NEW
HOLLAND

First published in 2011 by New Holland Publishers
London • Cape Town • Sydney • Auckland
www.newhollandpublishers.com

Garfield House, 86-88 Edgware Road, London W2 2EA, United Kingdom
80 McKenzie Street, Cape Town, 8001, South Africa
Unit 1, 66 Gibbes Street, Chatswood, NSW 2067, Australia
218 Lake Road, Northcote, Auckland, New Zealand

10 9 8 7 6 5 4 3 2 1

A CIP catalogue record for this book is available from the British Library.

ISBN 978 1 84773 692 5

Publisher: Simon Papps
Editor: Beth Lucas
Artwork: David Nurney
Production: Melanie Dowland

Reproduction by Pica Digital (Pte) Ltd, Singapore
Printed and bound in India by Replika Press Pvt. Ltd.

Contents

Foreword by Chris Packham 5

It's Coming Home ... We're Going Away 7
Spain, 1966

The Italian Little Brown Jobs 16
Italy, 1969

For Richer, For Birder 22
Mallorca, 1976

The Package Holiday Birder 29
Mallorca, 1984

Flycatcher Identification Stripped Bare 34
Crete, 1986

Nessun Birder 43
Mallorca, 1990

Two Countries Divided by a Single Language 54
California, 1991

East Side Story 71
New York, 1992

Walking in the Shadow of a Giant 78
Connecticut, 1995

The British are Coming 86
New Jersey, 1995

Rich Man, Poor Man 103
Gambia, 2000

The Girl Who Teaches Gorillas to Laugh 115
Cameroon, 2006

The Friendly Heart of Africa 124
Malawi, 2007

The Longest Drive 135
California, 2001

Howler 149
Arizona, 2003

Cape May Revisited 160
New Jersey, 1999

Stung into Action 176
Panama, 2005

Desert Colours 189
Israel, 1997

International Rescue 201
Cyprus, 2005

By Royal Appointment 209
The Falkland Islands, 2006

FOREWORD

Following hot off the press behind *Tales of a Tabloid Twitcher*, this 'confessions' sequel is equally as entertaining through its total and enthusiastic honesty. Stuart revels in the chaotic days of his early birdwatching abroad and entertains us with a rich catalogue of botched birding in bizarre and compromised scenarios. Whether it is his ribald excursions with his hysterical parents or more recently his own long-suffering family, he portrays a hugely entertaining catalogue of avian adventures experienced against the odds. Psychopathic Germans, incensed Dutch, bemused Spanish and confused Italians pepper his florid tales, not to mention the notorious 'Brits Abroad'. The strangest thing is that at times he did actually see some jolly good birds in some pretty unusual and spectacular places.

What makes it all such a good read is Stu's total 'great blokedness'. He has no snobbery and is happy to try any aspect of ornithology out for size. He is, perhaps, the ultimate polymath birder and while he may comment on the rest of us, and our peculiarities, he never stoops to judge even our most extreme or nonsensical pursuits. His writing is not only a pleasure to read but also hugely instrumental in bringing birding and its real concerns and crises to members of the public who otherwise would never engage with his and our passion. He is funny but he has a deeply serious commitment to extend an interest in birding to all. Because, as this madcap book certainly proves, chasing birds can be fun, if sometimes only with the benefit of hindsight!

I hope you enjoy these adventures as much as I did – such a pity that the *Carry On* romps have not lasted, as much of this would fit perfectly into *Carry On Birding*. Who would play Stuart though? Sid James, I fancy!

Chris Packham

PS Does anyone know whether he has seen a Puffin yet?

It's Coming Home …
We're Going Away
Spain, 1966

Football was coming home; the Winter family was heading abroad. If, as Philip Larkin suggested, 1963 was when sexual intercourse began, then the long, balmy summer of '66 was when England discovered how to lose its inhibitions completely and my family discovered the delights of sangria, sunburn and Spanish tummy. At home, skirts were rising faster than inflation; fusty barber shops morphed into groovy hairdressers, free love abounded and Carnaby Street was swinging like a pendulum on amphetamines

Meanwhile, a red, white and blue miasma was about to descend on the land, spawning the kind of jingoism not seen since the

Second World War. 'The Hun', to quote my dear father, would bear the brunt of patriotic fervour in the lead up to the eighth Jules Rimet Trophy, staged in the birthplace of football. There would be no Scots to pillory, but Dad would be sure to scream abuse at a youthful Franz 'Der Kaiser' Beckenbauer and his Teutonic teammates on the little black and white television in the corner of our front room. Dad's seismic explosions of fury at the slightest refereeing error, or any hint of foul play against 'his boys', as he liked to call the England team during televised matches, would surely see the wafer thin doors of our two-up-two-down council house peppered with punch marks.

The thought of 19 days of Kenneth Wolstenholme's and Hugh Johns' commentaries replacing *The Newcomers* and *Coronation Street*, as well as Dad's temper regularly rocketing off the Richter scale and threatening the very fabric of the house, was all too much for Mum. She booked a package holiday for the three of us on Spain's Costa Brava. Ironically, it was Dad's anti-German feelings that were to be a catalyst for my awakening to the beauty and excitement of birdwatching abroad.

A week's full-board package holiday was exotic. Most of our neighbours spent the three-week summer break camping in Rhyl or hiring caravans in Bognor. We were lucky. Mum and Dad worked at Vauxhall's massive Dunstable factory and I was their only child. Paying for a £60 all-in family getaway on the never-never was not too much of a hardship and, for Dad, whose wanderlust had only ever been fed by a trip to Belgium, missing the World Cup to experience Franco's Spain seemed a sacrifice worth making. Ernest Hemingway's accounts of brutal bullfights and the bloodletting of the Spanish Civil War were Dad's preferred bedtime reading and one of his favourite leisure activities was spreading a map of the Iberian Peninsula on the dining table to explain where the best fighting bulls were reared and where his heroes in the International

Brigade had fallen. Back then, I was still too young to know that Spain was also a wonderful place to watch birds.

At the age of ten, birds were just one of a handful of hobbies that kept me amused during those long summers when daylight never seemed to dim. Football kickabouts, stamp collecting and fighting mock battles in the fields that ringed our council estate were all enjoyable distractions from the horrors of school work. That year, I had endured the wrath of the most mean-spirited teacher of my entire education. He was a Second World War veteran who had lost all compassion and kindness in the sands of North Africa and he picked on me relentlessly. When the bell sounded on that last Friday of the school year and I knew that we would be flying out of Luton Airport to Spain within 24 hours, I instinctively felt, perhaps like Dad with his maps on the dining table, that travel and exploration were wonderful antidotes to the drudgery of everyday life.

That said, I remember very little of that summer holiday in Lloret de Mar. We flew out to Perpignan on a turbo-prop Britannia and then endured an arduous coach trip across the foothills of the Pyrenees into Spain, with regular stops for me to be sick. The first day, Dad acted all continental, saying he preferred rock-hard rolls with jam and coffee for breakfast to the Kellogg's cornflakes we had at home, while Mum seemed happy to put on a bikini after eyeing up all the XXXL-size 'foreign women', who commandeered the sunbeds hours before we rose each morning.

If Mum had thought a trip to Spain would calm Dad's occasional xenophobic outbursts against 'the enemy' she was misguided. Although she had lost her sister during the war to a Nazi flying-bomb directed at London's East End, it was Dad who still felt the pain and hatred more than 20 years after VE Day. He had been too young to fight but he had witnessed the carnage of the Blitz. His brother had also suffered terrible health problems after being demobbed from the army, which only exacerbated his bitterness against the old enemy.

By the age of ten I knew the *Observer's Book of Birds* by heart, largely because of Dad's patience in testing me when he got home from work each evening. Placing his hand over the bird names, he would ask me to identify different species from the beautiful Archibald Thorburn paintings. If I got them all correct, I received a 'joey' – the old Cockney name for a thruppenny bit. Putting my knowledge to the test in field conditions would have been an entirely different proposition. Even in the Sixties, when youngsters always walked to school and could wander all day without social services being alerted, I had never actually gone off looking for birds. There would be the occasional nature walk from school and Dad took me on regular route marches across local farmland, but these adventures were without binoculars or any idea of finding birds. Real contact with the living world was still confined to watching the tits and finches that visited our small home-made bird table. In truth, I had yet to develop a currency for birds. Penny Black stamps had an aura about them because of their monetary value. Looking through a neighbour's home-made telescope and seeing the moons of Jupiter created an indescribable thrill. Being allowed to stay up late to see the legendary Jimmy Greaves cut through Manchester United's defence on *Match of the Day* was awe-inspiring. But get excited about birds? I had once tried to turn a Carrion Crown into a Sparrowhawk by virtue of its fingered wings, and the appearance of a salmon-pink male Bullfinch on our rose bushes had been a thrilling experience, but I had not yet encountered anything coated in feathers that could create the adrenalin rush needed to get a youngster hooked. The Winters' first foreign adventure in Spain was to change that.

The story has been regaled so many times at family get-togethers over the decades that it has been imprinted in my memory banks. As with many Anglo-German rivalries, the genesis of the conflict was a series of trivial events that erupted into full-scale hostilities. The so-called Battle of the Costa Brava began as my parents were enjoying a relaxed after-dinner drink in the hotel's garden bar. Imagine the scene: a wasp-waisted waiter called Juan, lots of potted palms, flowering bougainvillea and a row of bottles full of the local firewater lined up along a Formica-topped bar. Mum was perched precariously on a stool, Dad standing by her side with a glass of fizzy beer while I was swinging gently on one of those chintzy hanging seats that were all the rage on patios both home and abroad. This scene of familial peace and calm was all too rudely interrupted by a drunken British holidaymaker, not one of the Union Flag shorts and string vest variety, but a Terry Thomas-lookalike with a pencil-thin moustache, plummy accent and a large glass of red wine. For all his correctly enunciated apologies as he drunkenly played pinball with the tables and chairs, it was obvious he was an accident waiting to happen, twice bumping into Dad and then a portly, bald-headed German who was also standing at the bar. On his third stumble, he cannoned off Dad, missed the German but managed to pour the entire contents of his glass over Mum. She screamed as her flowery yellow sundress was dyed Rioja red in an instant. The contrite drunk, anxious to make amends, decided to pick up a soda siphon from the bar and attempt a well-known DIY stain-removing procedure.

'Sozzy, my dear, zis is absolutely the very, very, very best way to get red wine stains out of pretty little frocks,' he drawled, before lining up the siphon's nozzle in entirely the wrong direction. One squirt set off World War Three. The flow of frothy white water missed Mum and her ruined dress, cascaded past Dad and hit the German full on the back of his bullet-shaped head.

'*Mein Gott!*' The German screamed like SS Storm-troopers always did in the *Victor* and *Hornet* whenever they were shot up by our Tommies. But the incensed man was far from done for. With a shake of his head, he came to his senses and proceeded to bring a flat hand down firmly on Mum's backside as she was still trying to attend to the drunk who had slithered to the floor like a discarded string puppet.

I half expected a torrent of ribald abuse from Mum, whose Cockney invective knew no bounds when it came to delivering rebukes, but the shock and pain had left her speechless. Not Dad, though.

'You bloody Kraut, take your hands off my missus,' Dad stormed, delivering a wild haymaker, which missed the German's lantern jaw but struck him full on the shoulder, sending the giant flying backwards across a cheap plastic table and leaving him squatting on a plant pot as if he was on the toilet. There was an unreal silence and then the German rose to his feet and flexed his biceps. His eyes went red and steam billowed from his ears. Dad took one look and scarpered into the night, his opponent in hot pursuit. He never caught up. Dunkirk, as Dad regularly reminded me over the years, was one of the greatest British military victories. Always better to run away and fight another day, were his favourite watchwords. It worked well that night. Twelve hours later it was my turn to do duty for Queen and country.

Dad's anti-German diatribe, which continued at the breakfast table with comments about women not shaving under their arms and men eating like pigs, left me wanting to continue hostilities against the Old Foe. I got my chance in a souvenir shop on the way to the beach later that morning. There, among the tourist tat of straw donkeys, sombreros and wine decanters, a smart elderly couple were engrossed in making a purchase. From the guttural tones of their conversation it seemed obvious they were speaking German. I confronted them.

'Heil Hitler!' I shouted, holding my arm up in a full Nazi salute and then clicking my heels before launching into the high-kicking march I had seen on the newsreels. The sight of a goose-stepping ten-year-old boy praising the most demented dictator in history was too much for the woman, who burst into tears. More guttural vowels and clipped consonants followed as the husband went berserk and chased me out of the shop, trying, no doubt, to administer some summary corporal punishment. Dad was outside waiting. He hated shopping as much as he hated the Germans and grown men picking on his only son.

He confronted the man, whose face had gone the colour of a beetroot. Speaking in perfect English, the man explained everything that had happened inside the shop from my Nazi salute to his wife's obvious distress. I could see Dad's face going equally red and soon sensed that my idea of anti-German solidarity was not to his liking. When he began raising his hands in a form of apologetic surrender I knew I was in trouble. It turned out the couple were Dutch and had lost relatives during the Nazi occupation of the Netherlands. They hated everything that Hitler and his cohorts stood for and had certainly not seen the funny side of a young English boy resurrecting the ghosts of a tragic era. Mum emerged from the shop in time to hear my Dad making a grovelling apology. As soon as the Dutch couple had departed, Mum turned on Dad.

'It's your bloody fault,' she scolded. Being brought up in the East End she could cuss with the best of them. 'Isn't it time you stopped being so juvenile and set an example for the boy? No wonder he's the way he is.' With that, Mum ruled there would be no 'fighting 'em on the beaches' that day and instead of sunbathing and making sandcastles, the three of us would go sightseeing. A boat trip to a neighbouring resort was her preferred option, a decision that would go on to shape my interest in birds for decades to come.

The boat trip from Lloret del Mar to nearby Blanes was unmemorable, apart from Dad bumping into an old school friend he had not seen for 20 years, but almost as soon as we made landfall something happened that I believe to this day is the reason why I love birds and birding. All birdwatchers have their rites of passage and such life-changing events can come any time and in many ways: seeing a Waxwing feast on a garden sorbus or watching a Peregrine swoop at unearthly speed; noticing a majestic Golden Eagle soaring over a heather-clad glen or opening the viewing hatch of a hide to gaze upon teeming masses of shorebirds. My epiphany came in an ornamental garden on a Costa Brava seafront after events that could so easily have seen me nursing a spanked backside or boxed ears.

My mind's eye still produces a high definition recall of the scene. There was a manicured lawn, strikingly verdant in the heat of an arid Mediterranean summer, and oleanders to add a dash of pastel pink. There was also a small picket fence and a 'keep off the grass' sign in Spanish, although this did not stop an interloper appearing from nowhere to flutter down on to the lush, irrigated sward. In an instant, I knew what it was – a Hoopoe! I had seen one before, albeit in monotone in my *Observer's Book of Birds*, but now it strutted before me, seemingly as pink as the flowers. I watched agog. There was so much to absorb: the crest, the droopy bill, the chequerboard wings. This was a mythical creature that could have come straight from the pages of *The Lion, the Witch and the Wardrobe*. I was transfixed. No bird I had seen before was either so beautiful or so magical.

Only when the Hoopoe picked up an insect and fluttered off on its moth-like wings of black and white was the spell broken. Or was it? Like Edmund, who became enchanted in Narnia by the White Witch's Turkish delight, I too was beguiled. The thrill of seeing such a rare bird was euphoric, like scoring a goal in a school football match or getting a star for homework. It was opening a Christmas present or tucking into an Easter egg; it was staying up late to watch television. I had been bewitched: the only cure was to see more exciting, exotic birds. In an instant, I had become an 'international' bird watcher, albeit one still in short trousers and with no binoculars.

For the record, Mum's plans to avoid the World Cup went awry. England won through the group stages, quarter and semi-finals and we arrived back home in time to see them beat Germany 4–2 in one of the most fraught sporting moments in history. The doors of the old house still bear the scars of Dad's excitement as the game slipped into extra time.

The Italian Little Brown Jobs
Italy, 1969

Whether due to fears of more Anglo–German diplomatic incidents or simply the economic woes of the Wilson era, the family's overseas adventures were put on hold for a few years. The next time we dared venture abroad Britain was still twelve months off from the fervour of the 1970 World Cup and, this time, my parents opted for a resort where battles for sunbeds would be unnecessary. The Italian Adriatic resort of Lido de Jesolo has one of the longest seafronts on the package traveller's itinerary – ten miles of golden sands and an equally lengthy ribbon of hotels, and arguably more sunbeds per square inch than anywhere else in Christendom to quell internecine squabbles between bathers from across the European landmass. By now, at the age of 13, I was in the early stages of developing into a 'bird watcher' (two words back in the late Sixties). I was still something of a fledgling: I had developed some contour plumage (my first pair of Prinz 10x50 binoculars, price £19) but my primaries were still developing (the farthest I had stretched my wings to see birds was a trip to the nearby Dunstable Sewage Farm). What I lacked in on-the-road experience I made up for in wanderlust.

Like Dad, I had become a map fanatic. Spreading out Ordnance Survey charts on the dining table or reading atlases in front of the fire was a substitute, albeit a somewhat unsatisfying one, for the in-the-field experiences I was so badly lacking. Instead, I made up pretend journeys to those wondrous places mentioned in the YOC magazine, *Bird Life*, and any other reading matter I could get my hands on about a hobby that was fast becoming a passion. When a package arrived from the Italian Tourist Board filled with information about Lido de Jesolo and its environs, I began drawing up imaginary plans for my first expedition overseas. The fold-up map of the resort nestling at the northern end of the Adriatic Sea screamed birds. Built on the seaward side of the vast Venetian Lagoon, with its shallow waters and brackish marshes, it seemed the resort had been constructed on the fringes of a giant Minsmere-like nature reserve, the size of an entire English county. Yet exactly which birds were there to see remained a mystery. This was the year before John Gooders published his groundbreaking *Where to Watch Birds in Europe* – a book that was to open up exotic continental birds to the masses – and I could only guess what wonders awaited. Not that I knew too many European species back in the late Sixties. I was still using my *Observer's Book of Birds* and anything else that I could borrow from the school's burgeoning ornithological library. A developing band of bird fanatics in my school year had become ever-hungry for new titles and the chance to discover species outside our regular orbit. One book in particular was very much in demand: Collins' *Field Guide to the Birds of Britain and Europe*.

On a few trips out with adult members of the local natural history society I had become mesmerised by this book, marvelling at Roger Tory Peterson's beautifully crafted plates and the mythical birds they displayed in glorious colour. There was my favourite, the Hoopoe, but now even its dazzling plumage was outshone by other more flamboyant apparitions – the Roller and Bee-eater. There was another bird that bore a slight resemblance to the Hoopoe but, rather than being dressed in tones of pink, the Wallcreeper shimmered like a ruby. The plate that carried pictures of Blackbird, Fieldfare and Redwing, birds that had all occurred in my garden, had a footnote section under the heading: 'some rare thrushes' with pictures of species I never knew I never knew. White's, Siberian, Naumann's, Dusky and Eyebrowed Thrushes – they might as well have lived on another planet. Only the American Robin seemed familiar, but this was more to do with Hollywood's miscasting of this North American thrush rather than European Robin for the 'Spoonful of Sugar' sequence in the Disney blockbuster, *Mary Poppins*.

Turning the pages revealed a display of 'swamp warblers', a nondescript collection of similar looking, small brown birds, most of which I had never heard of. Seeing and then identifying Savi's, Cetti's, Moustached, Great Reed and Fan-tailed Warblers was an elusive dream, a bit like having my own copy of the Collins guide, which at 30 shillings was well beyond the reserves of a depleted piggy bank. As the holiday approached, I came to terms with the fact that the Collins would not be going into one of the matching red suitcases, but at least Mum said I could take my binoculars as hand luggage as long as they were kept in their case while we travelled. A bird watching adventure was about to begin.

Looking through the grainy family photographs of that summer holiday 40 years on it seems that package breaks have hardly changed. Bikinis are more daring, sarongs have taken the place of towelling beach robes and today everyone looks catatonic, wearing headphones and lip syncin' as they slumber on loungers, but the basic ideology of sun, sand and a few other words beginning with S still make for the perfect two-week Mediterranean break. The photos show that our holiday in August 1969 comprised several 'S' activities: swimming, sunbathing, siestas and sightseeing. I can still remember going on the regulation gondola ride in Venice and getting coated in guano by the pigeons of St Mark's Square. I also remember falling in love with pizza decades before it became the favourite fare of couch potato society in the UK. And I remember my embryonic European list.

Each morning before breakfast, as Mum prepared for a day lounging on the beach, Dad would take me on a short walk around the fields and the lush riverside habitat of reed stands and bulrushes that skirted the resort. There were Blackbirds, Goldfinches and Greenfinches aplenty around the urban sprawl and Black-headed Gulls, Moorhens and Coots on the river, but soon it became obvious I was now watching birds on a new frontier. Bright little canary-like birds trilled on television aerials, white heron-like ghosts stalked the marshlands and countless little brown birds shinned up reed stems or skulked in the morass of sedges. Even the House Sparrows, with their chocolate coloured caps, looked so unlike the ones back home. Most remained frustrating blurs, and even when I managed to focus on any confiding individuals I was still perplexed. My prayers were soon answered. Sneaking off one night to read the English papers in a news-stand-cum-bookshop as my parents enjoyed a post-dinner drink – I was hooked on tabloids as soon as I could read – I stumbled across the solution to my confusion: the code-breaker, the bird watching Rosetta Stone, although frustratingly, it was in Italian. For a schoolboy who found conjugating French verbs difficult, trying to decipher an Italian edition of the Collins' European guide with bird names such as 'Cannaiola', 'Cannareccione', 'Forapaglie' and

'Capinera' seemed madness. They sounded more like the Italian national football team's back four than the species I had been seeing during our daily walks.

Not wishing to waste money on a book I could not read, I came up with a cunning ruse. Each day, on my birding walk with Dad, I would make matchstick sketches of birds I could not name in my notebook and then at night, while my parents were socialising with other hotel guests, I would go to the shop and match my little drawings with the pictures in the book. It worked! The buzzing bird that would bound across the scrubby margins of the lagoons on spring driven wings was a 'Beccamoschino'. I did not know its English name but by scribbling down its scientific Latin name next to my drawing I knew I would one day be able to make a positive ID back home. Slowly the likes of 'Airone bianco', 'Airone rosso', 'Usignolo di fiume', 'Pigliamosche' and 'Venturone' filled the pages of the exercise book. Little did I realise that I was teaching myself the golden principle of birding. Sadly, note taking is dying as an art form today. When was the last time you saw a birdwatcher making notes in the field?

On the last day of the holiday, Dad and I had time for a final walk by the slow-flowing River Piave before the coach arrived to take us back to the airport. More than 40 years on I can still smell the lush riverside vegetation warming under a new day's sun and picture Barn Swallows darting down to pick off insects from the mirror-like waters. A leisurely 'Falco di Palude' wafted by on flappy, fingered wings, creamy head and shoulders glistening in the early morning sunlight. I watched open-mouthed, my tummy doing cartwheels. This was a species I had long dreamed about, so much so that I not only knew the field marks but also its name in both English and Italian – it was the bird I had pored over longingly during my nightly trips to the book shop. Why did it so fascinate me? A week before going on holiday I had fallen in love with one sitting proudly in a display case at the local junkshop! For Falco di Palude, read Marsh Harrier.

Back in 1969 this was arguably Britain's rarest breeding raptor, confined to Minsmere and a few other secret locations. Family friends had told my parents about a 'stuffed eagle' for sale and I spent days gazing longingly at the bird through the shop glass pondering whether to spend my entire life savings − only three pounds, seven shillings and six pence was left after buying my bins − on such a curio. When I finally decided to hand over my cash, Dad, who had offered to drive me and the massive display case home, took one look and intervened.

'Sorry, son, you're not having that bloody thing in the house,' he grumbled. 'It's rotten, full of woodworm. They'll eat through the house in days. Your mother will go mad.' And so I left the Marsh Harrier behind, her forlorn glass eye looking at me wistfully. The old wooden display may have had a few telling pockmarks but it contained something of awe and wonder.

Standing by the Piave, I thought back to the junkshop and pondered how some Victorian maniac could have killed such a majestic creature. In some ways I was glad I had not bought the mounted specimen. Marsh Harriers were best enjoyed in the wild, not in a walnut veneered case. Anyway, there was something more important to do with my savings on my return home: buy the *Field Guide to the Birds of Britain and Europe*. Using the Italian and scientific names I had noted so diligently, I would finally be able to discover the English names for Airone bianco, Airone rosso, Usignolo di fiume, Pigliamosche and Venturone.*

*Airone bianco: Great Egret; *Airone rosso*: Purple Heron; Beccamoschino: Streaked Fantail Warbler; *Usignolo di fiume*: Cetti's Warbler; *Pigliamosche*: Spotted Flycatcher; *Venturone*: Serin; *Cannaiola*: Reed Warbler; *Cannareccione*: Great Reed Warbler; *Forapaglie*: Sedge Warbler; *Capinera*: Blackcap

For Richer, For Birder

Mallorca, 1976

I love the smell of sewage in the morning. I don't mean the raw, fetid stench that pervades poverty-stricken shanty towns or the overwhelming odour of student digs. Septic tanks make me heave and the mere thought of changing the nappy of any child other than my own starts a gagging reflex akin to a Fulmar impression. Yet allow a few molecules of part-treated human effluent to reach my smell sensors and I start salivating like Pavlov's dog – at the thought of waders.

Dunstable Sewage Farm is writ large in my birding career. It was there that I saw my maiden Green Sandpiper exploding out of a drainage ditch, all squeaky alarm calls and inky black underwing, and it was also there that I encountered my first Turnstones, their tortoiseshell summer garb almost the same colour as the congealed mass of human unmentionable they were pattering over after it had been baked to a crisp by the later summer sun. Sanderlings, Little Stints and a Pectoral Sandpiper also made their debut in my schoolboy notebooks after touching down on the sludgy settling beds; events permanently etched into my memory by the smells that accompanied their arrival. It is said that smell and memory are inextricably linked. Yes, Parfum de Dunstable Sewage Farm was the signature scent of my birding apprenticeship and it also played a serendipitous part in one of my first birding adventures abroad.

On 4 July 1976, two hundred years to the day that the American Congress voted to accept the Declaration of Independence, I was paying my own homage to the good ol' US of A. Where else but Dunstable Sewage Farm. I was on the trail of a strange gull that had been loitering around the four lagoons that stored water as part of the sewage farm's effluent cleansing process. The word was that it might be a Laughing Gull, not only a bird I had no idea how to identify if it hit me in the face, but one I had never even heard of before. Back then, Larid identification was still in its infancy, awaiting the forensic approach of gull guru Peter Grant, whose home patch at Dungeness had witnessed the first British record of Laughing Gull ten years before. With no American field guide to hand and no illustration of the trans-Atlantic wanderer to peruse (and, to be honest, still struggling with the basics of ageing the likes of Black-headed Gull), my hopes of nailing such a mega-rarity were forlorn.

Less than an hour after secreting myself inside the verboten sewage works, an operation that required either climbing over a barbed-wire fence or limbo-dancing underneath the heavy-barred main gates, the effort of looking for the American 'sea gull' became all too much. It was hot – this was the famous, scorching summer of '76 – and eau de sewage works was proving to be head-spinning rather than alluring. I gave up and began the slow walk home, thirsty and despondent. Within seconds my mood changed. There, spread out in the kerb, lay a crisp £10 note, the Queen's eye squinting in the sunshine. Tenners were a bit of a rarity in those days and for a cub reporter earning a pitiful £11-a-week, the parchment-like feel of the bank note was quite exhilarating; indeed, I was pondering whether it was better than finding a Laughing Gull. Seconds later, my mind was made up as I caught the shape and colour of another pristine £10 note a few dozen yards along the road. And then another. And another! In all, nine £10 notes had somehow materialised on a quiet country road where only farm vehicles, rat-runners and foot-weary birdwatchers ever passed. How had the equivalent of two months' salary found its way here? Was it hot money, the proceeds of some dastardly crime that had been hurriedly discarded? My mind was full of questions as I rolled the notes up and put them safely in the case of my Prinz 10x50s. Of all the questions, the only one with an answer was what was I going to do with this incredible windfall? As soon as I got home, I telephoned the police. A panda car arrived within 15 minutes.

'So where's the other one, son?' The brusque bobby asked as he counted out the nine notes and put them in a transparent evidence bag. I looked aghast.

'What do you mean?' I asked innocently.

'Come on, lad. You're not telling me that you haven't given yourself a wee reward,' the policeman said with a wink. The constable left with the money and a knowing look but I was to have the last laugh. Three months later, Dunstable Police Station called to say there had been no claimants for the cash and so it was mine to spend as I so desired. A holiday beckoned – a bird watching one.

If one person inspired me to travel to see birds then it was the late John Gooders, whose contribution to modern birding should never be underestimated. Sadly, as I write these paragraphs I have just learned of the great man's untimely death, a passing that hopefully will be widely acknowledged by the birding community with some monument for his modernisation of a pastime that was steeped in Edwardian anachronisms. John Gooders' prolific writing during the Seventies and Eighties inspired many to pick up binoculars, pack their passports and explore a world ripe for discovery. The groundbreaking and encyclopaedic *Birds of the World* he edited for several years remains one of my most treasured possessions and, even 40 years on, I can still sense that boyish adrenalin rush when it was pushed through the letter box every Friday along with the morning papers. While my *Birds of the World* were kept in pristine condition in the family bookcase, another of his publications, *Where to Watch Birds in Britain and Europe*, became dog-eared and tea-stained as I spent hour-upon-hour sprawled on the front room floor with it and a road atlas working out imaginary journeys to exotic birding locations. This truly inspirational work was essential reading in my teenage years, a classic to compete with *Lord of the Rings*, *Catch-22* and Kafka's *Trial*, yet when the inexhaustible Mr Gooders first penned his guide to finding little-known birds from the snowy Norwegian wastes of Varanger Fjord to the last known haunts of the Andalusian Hemipode in southern Spain, I guess he never thought it would be used for finding the ideal honeymoon location.

Fresh out of journalism college, earning only a pittance and with a wedding on the horizon, the £90 burning a hole in my pocket could easily have gone on curtaining, pots and pans, the latest toaster or a stag do. Instead, I scrutinised every page of the European *Where to Watch* guide seeking the perfect, tranquil getaway for newlyweds. And one that came with an exciting bird list, too. Rather than sticking to the tradition of keeping the honeymoon venue a secret, I explained everything to my fiancée Anne the day after confirming the booking, safe in the knowledge that north-east Mallorca, a place that looked excellent for birds, was also regarded as one of the most beautiful, romantic backdrops on the planet with its turquoise seas, sparkling white beaches and stunning vistas. Hollywood superstar Grace Kelly and Prince Rainier of Monaco had chosen the exclusive five-star Formentor Hotel, across the bay from our more humble but equally charming – and 'birdier' – quarters.

For an island that has suffered all the worst excesses of the package holiday revolution, everything from imported beer, all-day breakfasts, dusk-to-dawn electronic dance music and high-rise hotels to overweight men in thongs, the charming resort of Puerto Pollensa has managed to retain much of its charm. Back in the autumn of 1976, the one-time fishing village had been little troubled by the mass tourism that has gone on to despoil so much of the largest island of the Balearic archipelago. Hotels were situated perfectly for long daytime walks and intimate candlelit dinners. Within seconds of leaving the hotel foyer, the Mediterranean's unique aromas – thyme-scented garrigue and sweet-smelling pines – delighted the senses, while the island's rocky spine of imposing limestone crags drew even honeymooners to go exploring.

Looking for postcards in a local souvenir shop the day after our arrival, I stumbled across the key to the island's hidden treasures: expat Eddie Watkinson's excellent *Guide to Birdwatching in Mallorca*, a slim black-and-white paperback full of maps and hiking tips as well as locations for the island's headline birds. One venue soon stood out – the Boquer Valley, a migrant trap seemingly carved into the rocks and with a mouth-watering list of potential birds.

Early the next morning Anne and I packed a picnic lunch of local cheeses and cold meats, freshly baked bread and a tasty local speciality called *ensaimada*, a cross between a croissant and a cake, and began the long meandering stroll out of Puerto Pollensa towards the rocky crags that cast such an imposing shadow over the resort. We walked through sun-parched fields and an olive grove full of ancient gnarled trees, before passing through a farm courtyard where a mother cat lay suckling her litter of tortoiseshell and marmalade kittens. Using the Watkinson guide book, we continued along an ancient goat track until we found ourselves amid a collection of weirdly contorted, tooth-like rocks that appeared as if they had been worked on by quack dentists, still blissfully unaware of what we were about to witness. Only those who have been enchanted by the grandeur of the Boquer Valley will understand its first moment of captivation. Even for honeymooners caught up in their own little world, this most enthralling of wild places simply took our breath away. Blue skies, a warm breeze and the soft lilting tones of a Blue Rock Thrush echoing through the valley's yawning expanse made for an impression that is still as vivid in my mind today as it was on that special October morning four decades ago. Blend the rattling of Sardinian Warblers, flashing fiery Black Redstart tails and the sweeping shape of Peregrines into the collage of memories, and the moment was sealed forever in my heart. Then came one more moment of total enrapturement. A Hoopoe, the same bird that had so beguiled me in Spain a decade before, the same bird I had shown Anne on one of our very first dates at the Houghton Regis chalk quarry, flew languidly across the valley floor, radiating brilliant white flashes from its gingham-like wings.

Over the following days, we blazed the traditional tourist trail of local markets and sightseeing spots, as well as walking around our resort where Chiffchaffs and Robins were arriving in their hundreds ahead of the European winter. One bird, however, remained elusive – the mythical Eleonora's Falcon. October was supposedly the prime time to see this elegant hunter wreaking terror among passerines heading south to their African winter quarters. The falcon, itself a summer visitor from distant Madagascar, has a unique survival strategy, delaying nesting until early autumn so that it can capitalise on the abundance of migrant birds to feed its young.

Despite several views of scythe-shaped wings sweeping over the wilder parts of the island, I was too inexperienced to make a positive identification, and on a booked excursion to the falcon's stronghold, the precipitous cliffs of the Formentor peninsula, the weather was too wet and windy even to get out of the coach. On our final day and with the sun finally breaking through after almost 48 hours of continuous rainfall, I somehow managed to persuade Anne to give up the idea of simply chilling on the beach to visit one of Mallorca's 'most scenic and unspoilt landscapes', to quote some imaginary tourist bumf I had purportedly been reading. After six days of married life, I was already learning the subterfuge of a birdwatching cad, promising where we were heading boasted some of the finest sands across the whole Balearic island complex. Suitably impressed, Anne and I set off for the S'Albufera, the vast wetland that proved as difficult to bird watch that day as it did for the burgeoning tourist industry to develop over subsequent years. Impenetrable reed beds stretched across the flat, coastal plain as far as the eye could see and, apart from a few gulls – Yellow-legged Gulls were still not in my lexicon – and patrolling Marsh Harriers, the area appeared bereft of birds.

There were countless mercurial LBJs – little brown jobs – but these were far beyond my knowledge of the finer points of *Acrocephalus* identification criteria as well as my practical field skills. For all Watkinson's plaudits for the site and my expectations that it would be the Mallorquin equivalent of Minsmere, the place seemed both unworkable and unwalkable. The long, energy-sapping hike there and back in warm autumn temperatures (I had promised it was only a 'short amble') almost ended our marriage after less than a week. Several decades later Anne still uses the agonies she endured on the 'Great Walk to S'Albufera' as an excuse to get out of joining me on birding strolls.

The Package Holiday Birder
Mallorca, 1984

Eight years would pass before my serotonin levels were once again boosted by Mediterranean sunshine and my head was turned by the shapes and bright colours of exotic birds that for too long had remained tantalising illustrations in field guides. Those eight years had also seen two major changes in my life. I had become a father of two daughters – and I had become a birder. Emily was born in October 1981 and Charlotte almost two years to the day later. A little more than 18 months before Emily's birth, I had experienced my birdwatching epiphany.

The date was 22 March 1980. I had joined an RSPB local members' group trip to Walberswick and realised that the occasional saunter to my beloved sewage farm or a walk around Tring Reservoirs were never going to provide true fulfilment. To be a real 'birder' – this imported Americanism had begun to gain favour among the masses during the late Seventies – I needed to stretch my wings, to explore the gorse-clad heaths of the New Forest for Dartford Warblers and Woodlarks or journey to the beautiful oak woods of the Forest of Dean, where the songs of Wood Warbler, Common Redstart and Pied Flycatcher resonated amid the rustling of leaves. There were also seas to scan with my brand new Optolyth telescope. But, most of all, there was the call of the wild Norfolk coast and the allure of straggling vagrants from all points of the compass: wildfowl and waders from across the Atlantic and warblers from the distant forests of Siberia.

Yet, as my life list blossomed with the likes of Surf Scoter, Baird's Sandpiper and Yellow-browed Warbler, my eyes and dreams were always focussing southwards. That first encounter with the Hoopoe as a ten-year-old, along with the still-vivid memories of walks with my father on the fringes of the Venetian Lagoons, had fired the desire to travel abroad to watch birds; our honeymoon on the jewel of Balearics had intensified the longing to see those southern European birds famed for their bright colours and tantalising summer habits of overshooting their nesting grounds in warm climes for Britain. Bee-eaters and Rollers, Woodchat Shrikes and Subalpine Warblers, Great Spotted Cuckoos and Red-rumped Swallows, these glittering gems of the Mediterranean exuded Latin flair, their plumage tones flying off the pages of field guides to provide that ceaseless feeling of expectancy that drives every birdwatcher to venture forth.

Such sensations had been bubbling inside me from the moment the family had booked a one-week break at a sprawling new-build development on the outskirts of Alcudia, the neighbouring resort to Puerto Pollensa. One can only speculate – and grieve over – what wonderful habitat had been destroyed to create a complex that looked as if had been dropped from the outskirts of an industrial town behind the Iron Curtain on the bejewelled shores of the northern Mallorcan coast, but for a young family on a limited income it offered a cheap holiday in the sun.

Sunshine, unfortunately, was in short measure in the spring of May 1984. Our arrival heralded non-stop rain and cool northerlies, weather conditions that had Anne vowing never to take a mid-spring break again, but also created a climatic hurdle for tired migrants on the last leg of their journey from Africa to Europe. Looking through rain-spattered apartment windows at the swirling grey skies and wind-lashed trees, one could sense the frustrations of hormone-driven hirundines and warblers held up on their great flight north. I was fretting, too; pinned down by the weather and having to keep a young family occupied in cramped conditions when the beach – and birds – should have been beckoning. Almost two days of cabin fever passed in an instant when a break in the weather meant four bleak white walls could finally give way to fresh air and the sweeping grandeur of Alcudia's sandy bay. I could also attempt that most challenging of roles: Birding Dad.

Juggling the needs of a family against the gravitational pull of birds demands superhuman skills: diplomacy, patience, anticipation, time management and subterfuge. Trial and error over the years has taught me how to be both dutiful and diligent for the family and yet still surreptitiously build a bird list. Such skills were still in their infancy that year, but I learned fast. By the time I had created a beach camp with windbreak, sunbeds and parasol; strategically arranged towels; paddled in a chilly sea with excited children; ferried cans of pop and coffees from the beach bar; constructed a sandcastle of Windsor Castle-like proportions and persuaded everyone to take a pre-lunch nap, I was free...

That first walk alone on foreign soil with telescope and tripod draped across my shoulders and a pair of trusty Jenoptem 8x30 binoculars pressed satisfyingly against my chest unfurled such feelings of excitement, such a spirit of anticipation. Never before had I been free to bird abroad without being under the watchful gaze of a parent or having to be aware of a partner's sensibilities.

At the time I was working on a book called *Best Days with British Birds*, an anthology of stories from leading birdwatching figures and, despite the domestic nature of the title, believed that it would also include accounts of travels abroad and encounters with foreign birds. With this in mind, I made a few hurried scribbles in my log, thinking these would help if ever I needed to write the full story of my first real overseas birding adventure. To experienced travellers, the following extract may seem very mundane, but to this day I can still feel the sun on my back and hear the jangling Serins.

Hoorah! Freedom! I don't think I have been so excited about going birding in my life. I left Anne and the kids on the beach for a few hours this morning while I ventured inland and pottered around the waste ground at the back of the resort. The place was a tip. Rubbish and bits of building detritus – even a few dead dogs. It seems as if the site was going to be developed but somehow the building work has stopped and the ground is reverting back to nature. The birds don't mind. It's funny how so-called waste ground is so often birdier than protected pristine habitats. Here's no exception.

It was great to feel the sun beating down after all the rain and the butterflies were out in force. Glad I've brought the MB [Mitchell Beazley] 'butty' guide because one of the first b'fs I saw was new to me – a Cleopatra. Wonderful. Butter-coloured like a Brimstone, with what looks like two dabs of peach jam on the forewing. Could have spent all my time looking downwards but there was too much going on above. Serins were everywhere, tinkling like miniature Corn Buntings from every available perch. Wish the Sardinian Warblers were equally demonstrative. They skulk through the scrub with their black hoods looking like bank robbers. One male performed a song-flight, the white tips of his tail spread out like a Spanish fan, and when he landed he stared at me aggressively with his little red eye.

Out in the middle of the scrub was a male Woodchat, sitting calm and contented. Never moved all the time I was mooching about. Got brilliant scope views. It did not have a white patch at the base of the primaries like in the Peterson Guide.

A couple of Kentish Plovers (another new bird for me) have swapped the beach for a patch of open, sandy ground cleared by the bulldozers. How ironic that the holiday industry that has driven them from the shoreline is now helping find a new place to pitter-patter around like little biscuit-coloured clockwork toys. The male was particularly smart with his black collar studs and rusty cap. I thought they may have a nest – well, a scrape in the ground, to be accurate – so I was very careful where I put my feet.

The only disappointment of the morning was not being able to identify a largish falcon that I picked up in the distance. Seemed too large for Hobby and too rakish for Peregrine. I bet it was Eleonora's. Looks like I've dipped again.

Not seeing Eleonora's Falcon that holiday was a disappointment to be weighed against all the excitement of the other new birds that came my way: the White-winged Black Terns I saw from the famous 'Orange Bridge' floating effortlessly over the S'Albufera's brackish lagoons; the gangly Purple Heron with its heavy crop and outlandish feet; garrulous Black-winged Stilts that seemed so affronted whenever you raised your binoculars to watch them balance on their ridiculous supermodel-thin legs. There was also time to return to the Boquer, a pilgrimage to a place that had been scorched forever into my psyche. To feel the warm zephyrs dancing over the rocky, thyme-scented ground and hear stammering Cirl Buntings sounding almost embarrassed as their one-note songs competed against the operatic arias of a Blue Rock Thrush high on its craggy perch, left me vowing to return...

Flycatcher Identification
Stripped Bare
Crete, 1986

The Winter clan's travels continued apace after that first incursion overseas. By 1986, I was working in Fleet Street as a crime reporter for *Today* – Eddie Shah's revolutionary all-colour newspaper – which meant domestic finances could stretch to a hotel rather than self-catering apartment. We also spread our horizons a little further, exchanging the soft, sun-kissed sands of Mallorca for the coarse, rocky shores of Crete. Our minds had been made up by the intriguing and highly addictive late Seventies television drama series *Who Pays the Ferryman?* and the publication of Stephanie Coghlan's guide to the island's birding locations.

With a pushchair that had already seen service in the rockiest reaches of Mallorca, we set off on a package break that all too quickly became the equivalent of an intensive training programme for the SAS. So much for a hotel! The local goats would have found sleeping in our shabby, mosquito-infested accommodation not only demeaning but beyond their rock-climbing skills. Perhaps we were fortunate to be perched at the top of a rickety set of stairs because each night the other guests, a group of flabby middle-aged guys from some northern mining town, would hold noisy drinking parties around the grimy swimming pool until the sun rose. Their skimpy swimwear, set off by rolling lava fields of flab, seemed in keeping with the hotel's 'earthquake chic' decor.

Then there was the food. Getting the children to eat anything other than chips and cucumber from Cretan menus dominated by octopus and squid was a challenge that Hercules would have found beyond his strength and guile. The Ancient Greek superhero may have cleaned the Augean Stables in a day but he never had to persuade a five-year-old that a meal-time tangle of pink squidgy tentacles with suckers was really spaghetti. The biodiversity on our plates was matched by what we found in our room. Luckily, I had read before we left that Crete had no venomous snakes otherwise the sight of a slithering but harmless Leopard Snake, rattling its tail like a deadly American Eastern Diamondback Rattlesnake, would have been a wholly different experience when we discovered it secreted in our bedroom. How a three-foot snake had navigated the four dozen stairs was anyone's guess. Perhaps it had been brought in by one of the children, who had suddenly developed a liking, if not a taste, for the local fauna.

'Daddy, Daddy... Me got pet!' three-year-old Charlotte screamed excitedly one afternoon, waking me from a deep siesta by dangling a bright green Praying Mantis, front legs drawn up southpaw style, full in my face. I froze, not knowing whether the insect, with its

squinting face giving the Mike Tyson 'eyeball', would bite my
daughter or attack me. 'Put Mr Daddy-longlegs down like a good
girl. I don't think he wants to play today,' I whispered, before
ushering the six-inch long monster out the door with a flip-flop.

One invertebrate disposed of safely; others were to prove more
problematic. We still talk about the Curse of the Killer Crete
Mosquitoes. Sprays and plug-in deterrents were no match for the
whining horde who attacked throughout the night. By the end of
the holiday, my other daughter Emily was peppered with more than
100 red bites that blossomed like Manchester United rosettes across
her whole body. Much to her embarrassment as a grown woman, we
still have the photos to prove just how vengeful Cretan mosquitoes
can be when you've tried to poison, electrocute or flatten them with
a rolled up English newspaper. One can only guess what social
services would say about it nowadays.

We were finally rescued from mosquito hell by an influx of
Moorish Geckos, but for all the complaints about Crete's
invertebrate and reptile biodiversity, the birds on this part of the
island were a wonderful mix of Eastern specialities and Central
European autumn migrants stone-stepping across the
Mediterranean on their journeys south. Even in late September the
heat was so intense that any birding had to be compressed into a
two-hour session that began the moment the first shimmer of the
sun's corona emerged above the dawn horizon. There must be
hundreds of birdwatching dads who have had to balance spousal
holiday duties against the lure of new habitats and the promise of
exciting birds that come as unadvertised extras with a package
holiday abroad. Over the years I've met many a clock-watching
birder enjoying a couple of hours' first-light birding before going
back to sandcastle making, souvenir shopping with the missus or
trying to entice moody kids to eat calamares by pretending they are
really onion rings, so that family feng shui remains positive.

For the first few mornings, outings were confined to exploring the scrubby maquis that skirted the hotel and scrambling up rocky goat tracks trying to find the frustrating source of the 'chukar-chukar-chukar' calls that rippled among the boulders. Crested Larks with their haunting 'here, guess who' calls, rattling Sardinian Warblers and indigo-coloured Blue Rock Thrushes willingly threw themselves into binocular view, but the noisiest of all the hillside's inhabitants remained elusive. Only on the third morning did I get to grips with Chukar, almost killing myself in the process.

The friendly nature of the locals was a feature of every morning walk. Cretans hold the British in high esteem for the sacrifices made by the Allies during the fierce hand-to-hand fighting with Nazi paratroops in 1941, a brutal page in world history that has instilled such hatred among the islanders that German tourists were supposedly still being refused entry into some of the more remote mountain villages back in the mid-Eighties. Locals had no problems identifying me as a Brit. My puffy ankles, lobster colouring and baggy shorts left no doubts that I possessed a UK passport. Wizened goatherds with dark, leathery skin the same colour and texture as their waistcoats would greet you with cheery cries of 'kalimera' and open-mouthed grins, displaying teeth the colour of tortoiseshell combs. However, although the natives were friendly, the same could not be said about their dogs.

'Avoid all dogs abroad' is as important a tip for the travelling birder as 'bring your passport' and 'don't forget your binoculars'. No matter that we are a nation of dog lovers in the UK. On the whole, the positive feelings are generally reciprocated by man's best friend on home soil, but the message has not been passed on to canines on the continent. In most places abroad, the mutts fortunately still have a begrudging respect, or fear, of humans; overseas farm dogs, though, especially those built like brick outhouses and with spiked collars and fangs to match their size, invariably see human interlopers as potential meals. The word seems to have got round that birdwatchers are particularly tasty.

Dropping your guard, especially when in pursuit of a good bird, is easy and I fell into the trap – literally – when what looked like a rusty-tailed Long-legged Buzzard slowly glided over a hillside and then tantalisingly out of view. I was so intent on relocating the buzzard that I never saw the three large brutes savouring my scent. One hellish bark grabbed my attention, sending my fright and flight mechanisms haywire. Should I stand and throw stones or run and find some form of shelter? My hesitation meant the beasts were soon half a football pitch away – and closing. I ran towards a stone wall for all my worth, praying it might just prove too big for the dogs to clamber over.

Crash! In my blind panic, I had not seen a wispy strand of barbed wire poking out of the soil. The snare bit as hard as a Roy Keane tackle, sending me sprawling, limbs and tripod splayed like some weird seven-legged creature. I rolled into a ball, by now expecting the dogs to begin sinking their fangs into the few remaining parts of my body not wracked with pain. The bites never came. Instead, the commotion, a mixture of my screams and the dogs' frenzied barks, sent a covey of Chukars exploding into the air, their harsh calls drowning out the baying hounds. As I came to my senses, I could see the dogs held in a line 30 or so metres away. Between us was a deep gorge, far too wide for them to leap. Nothing was broken. Bins and scope had survived the tumble. My limbs were still in one piece, but my face, arms and legs were ripped raw. Even the sigh of relief hurt as I celebrated my escape from a savaging and the addition of Chukar on to my life list.

For the remainder of the holiday dog-free zones were at a premium. Farmsteads and villas were given a wide berth and, whenever I went out, I filled my pockets with a few conker-sized stones just in case of a confrontation with a stray. By now well into the holiday, I worked out a well-oiled routine for my morning adventures: I met a taxi driver who timed his early runs along the coast road so he could drop me off on the outskirts of the quaint fishing village of Elounda and then return two hours later.

Away from the traditional white-painted buildings, yacht-filled marina and restaurants decorated with newspaper cuttings harking back to the aforementioned BBC drama that had first put the port on the map, the landscape was stippled with olive trees. Working the twisting lanes that divided the olive groves and then peering surreptitiously over the grey stone walls at regular intervals seemed the best birding strategy. Sprinklings of late September migrants were filtering through the island, and the ancient trees with their twisted limbs coated in evergreen foliage seemed to be pulling tired warblers and flycatchers looking for respite out of the sky.

The genus *Phylloscopus* derives its name from the Greek *phyllo* meaning 'leaf' and *scopus* 'to watch' and some of its best known members, Chiffchaffs, Wood and Willow Warblers, were well at home, adding their own verdant hues to the drier, bluey-green tones of sun-bleached olive leaves they were scouring for food. Goldfinches and Greenfinches bickered and flickered among the parched under-storey that had long turned to straw, their startled movements becoming an annoyance as I tried to concentrate on getting good views of the countless *Ficedula* flycatchers that were trying to claim air superiority over the olive groves' insect population. Every snag, every exposed branch, was being used as a launch pad for their dashing sallies, which always began with a flash of white from their wings, a whirl of feathers and then invariably a muted 'click' as mandibles snapped shut on some unfortunate flying bug. Watching the life-or-death dogfights was enthralling; putting names to individual flycatchers a headache. My field skills were simply not up to the job of separating the Pieds, Collareds and Semicollared Flycatchers that must all have been represented but were all now adorned with their near-identical autumn garb of drab grey-brown upperparts and wing patterns the colour and complexity of *The Times* crossword. The birds would not perch long enough to detect if they had white primary bases or double wing-bars. Trying to work out tertial patterns was bringing on a migraine. Luckily, the olive groves came to an abrupt end and the land opened out into a flat, coastal sweep, shimmering with what I first took to be a mirage but then realised was a series of lagoons. Open water. I was in my comfort zone. I smelt birds.

There cannot be a saltpan anywhere in the Mediterranean that has not brought a smile to a visiting birder. Heat haze apart, they are perfect places to put up a scope and enjoy the spectacle produced by shallow water and rich supplies of invertebrates. For migrating waders, terns, gulls and wildfowl, they are vital service stations on the long journeys from Europe to Africa. The pans at Elounda were on the avian equivalent of the M25.

The dank, marshy margins of the saltpan complex were even birdier. Oozy vegetation was teeming with tip-toeing Yellow Wagtails, each one so individually marked that assigning them to any subspecies was impossible. There were none of the smart males in their dandy spring costumes present. Most were juveniles. Some had a hooded effect that made me think they would develop into the striking males of the Black-headed *feldegg* subspecies, others were just too variable to call. As I tried to get a closer view, a small pipit exploded into the sky from under my feet, offering a thin, high-pitched squeak before landing in the denser grass, its stripy plumage providing perfect camouflage. Its call meant one thing: a Red-throated Pipit, a new bird for me. I made another attempt to get close but the pipit was having none of it. Again, it took to the sky with a thin squeal before vanishing back into the damp grass. We began a dance of the hunter and hunted. The pipit was a formidable foe, not once allowing me a view of it on the ground. I could not justify flushing it again and with my watch showing that my early-morning birdwatching 'visa' was about to expire, I headed back to the rendezvous with the taxi driver. En route, I would be in for one more 'eye-opening' encounter.

Before reaching the shady olive grove with its squadrons of flycatchers on active service, I was brought suddenly to a halt by the smooth tones of a female English accent. Birders regularly get accosted by angry farmers or snotty security guards, but this voice was almost apologetic.

'Excuse me, can you tell me what you are doing? And what's that?'

I turned to find a woman pointing at my telescope and tripod. Before I could give an explanation my tongue dribbled out of my mouth as if it was melting ice cream. There in front of me stood a beautiful, honey-toned goddess with flowing raven hair and not a single item of clothing. Neither was there a single white mark to mar the uniformity of her all-over golden tan. My eyes wanted to study her every contour as if she was a perched flycatcher. Discretion held that I should only make eye contact.

'I'm birdwobbling.' My tongue had not retracted fully. Speaking coherent English was proving impossible.

'You're what?' said Aphrodite's long-lost sister, totally oblivious to the effects her nudity were having on my powers of speech.

'I'm birding... Looking at the birds! Honest.' I said apologetically, thinking she was going to accuse me of being some sort of sordid voyeur.

She sensed my discomfort and approached me. I squirmed.

'Can I have a look?' She purred like a seductive siren.

'Er... Er...' I must have sounded panic stricken. For a second, I

41

thought I was trapped in some sort of adult game of 'you-show-me-yours-I'll-show-mine', the kind kids play behind bicycle sheds before they're taught the facts of life.

'I mean your camera, silly,' the goddess smiled, pointing towards my scope.

'Oh, it's a telescope. It's for watching birds.' My tongue had almost returned to normal speech mode. 'I was looking at the birds on the saltpans. There are some good birds about.'

I did not know whether to end the sentence with 'honest' to emphasise that my behaviour was entirely innocuous, but instead decided to prove my birding story credible by focussing the scope on a small flock of Yellow-legged Gulls loafing on the water.

The young woman peered through the eyepiece. I stood behind not quite knowing where to direct my eyes. Her peach shaped bottom moved rhythmically as she tried to get into a comfortable viewing position. She was struggling with the focus.

'Here, I'll help,' I said, moving forward but taking care not to make any form of contact. I adjusted the focus wheel and she gave a reassuring sigh.

'This is amazing. I can see those seagulls as if they were in front of me.'

It did not seem right to go into the complexities of gull nomenclature, or mention that 'seagull' is a no-no word among birders. After scanning the horizon, she stood up and thanked me once more and then vanished back into the olive grove. Although I had given her a full account of what I was doing, I felt that she also had some explaining. Exactly what was a young English beauty doing on the edges of a saltpan at 8 a.m. – without a single stitch of clothing on?

'Women! They're more complex than flycatcher identification,' I thought to myself before heading off to the waiting taxi.

Nessun Birder

Mallorca, 1990

Italia 1990. Gazza's World Cup. The Three Lions and their raggle-taggle army of fans had miraculously found themselves in Turin on a warm night in early July. A struggle through the group stages had been followed by David Platt's last minute Bologna ace against Belgium and Gary Lineker's quarter-final penalty double against the Indomitable Lions of Cameroon. Now the old foe lay ahead. Beat Jurgen Klinsmann's West Germans and England would be in their first World Cup final since '66. John Barnes' rapping summed up the mood of the nation:

We ain't no hooligans
This ain't a football song

Three lions on my chest
I know we can't go wrong...

The whole country was praying for England. At home, millions were sweating and fretting. As in 1966, the Winters were going abroad to escape the jingoism and blood pressure-raising activities of eleven men dressed in white on a football field. A quarter century after my mother had ordered the family to up sticks to Spain prior to the big kick-off for Sir Alf Ramsey's pursuit of glory, Anne had decided on the same strategy: a family break overseas. Rather than mainland Spain, as my parents had chosen, Italia '90 would see us heading for the resort where we had honeymooned and taken the children as babies. I needed little persuasion. Even though spring migration was long over, early July still promised an attractive array of resident breeding birds in some of the more remote areas of Mallorca I had yet to explore. As an extra, there would also be plenty of sports bars to watch World Cup matches on the big screen with plenty of German tourists to ridicule. There was one added advantage: I was now in possession of an International Driver's Licence and the family budget could stretch to a hire car.

The previous summer's holiday on the Costa del Sol, a highly forgettable affair consisting largely of tummy bugs, lethargy-inducing summer temperatures, incessant timeshare punters and only one new bird, Black Wheatear, has been confined to the Holidays in Hell section of the Winter family archives. Unquestionably, the most harrowing incident involved my introduction to the joys of driving abroad. The idea of hiring a car had seemed so exotic and I can still feel the rush of excitement when the hotel reception rang our room to say the vehicle had arrived. Vehicle was a loose term. More a hairdryer on wheels than a family run-around, there was hardly enough room for two adults and two children and it was also the most appalling shade of brown, a colour that was to prove quite appropriate from the moment I picked up the keys and signed away my life.

'Ah, one thing, senor,' said the moustachioed hire car delivery agent with the kind of fiendish grin of a pantomime baddie. 'Zere is no gas in ze car. We give you tres extra days' hire for zis, how do you say, inconvenience. Ze gas station is just down the road.'

Just down the road, hmm. Four hours after setting off to top up the tennis ball-sized petrol tank with a couple of litres of fuel, I pulled back into the hotel car park white-haired, shaking, nails bitten to the quick and a reception committee of my distraught wife, crying children, the entire hotel management and two Civil Guard.

'We thought you were dead,' were Anne's first words as I stepped out of the vehicle and kissed the ground in an act of relief and gratitude for my deliverance. 'The hotel called the police out. They thought you had either been killed or kidnapped.'

I was so parched I could not speak. Cracked lips pleaded for water... then something stronger to calm my shattered nerves. Only when the Civil Guard had sped off to do some real policing with the hotel manager muttering in their ears about the 'loco Inglés' could I regale my horror story in full. The two-minute test drive around the hotel car park may have given me a cursory idea of changing gears with my right hand and getting used to the clutch control, but it had in no way prepared for me driving on Spain's notorious 'Calle de Muerte' otherwise known as the Road of Death. Back in the Eighties this blood-drenched ribbon of concrete meandered its malevolent way from Malaga Airport and through the bustling heart of the Costa del Sol's major tourist centres creating carnage. Many British tourists forgetting to reverse-wire their Green Cross Code would step out blindly into the path of oncoming traffic. UK motorists in their own right-hand drive vehicles or, like me, in hire cars would get confused about making a left-hand turn with tragic results.

Turning out of the hotel had been like pulling straight on to the M1 from a side road. Vehicles were shooting past me at 70 mph with only the thickness of a matador's cape between their respective bonnets and boots. At the sight of the first gap, I pushed my foot down on the spongy accelerator and prayed. A cacophony of car horns and contemptuous hand signals, meanings of which I had gleaned by watching Spanish footballers insulting their opponents, were hurled at me as I spluttered along at the kind of speed more associated with donkey carts. My whitened knuckles had to be prised off the steering wheel by the pump attendant when I finally found a garage to top up the tank. But that was just the start of the nightmare. I had to find a way of crossing over the central reservation to return to the hotel.

Pulling out once again on to the N-340 I was greeted with the same derision by the local drivers while I drove slowly enough to be able to do the equivalent of a U-turn as soon as possible. The opportunity never came and I just drove mile after mile after mile, confused and frightened by a road system I just could not work out. Gibraltar's mighty rocky edifice was looming in the distance by the time I found a traffic system that allowed me to make a 180 degree turn and begin the long trek back to the hotel, a journey that soon required another visit to another petrol station. The following day we took the children to Gibraltar to see its famous colony of macaques and also for me to sneak off for a few moments to scan the Rock's arid slopes for Barbary Partridge, the only place in mainland Europe this North African species occurs. We decided to set off at 4 a.m. to miss the traffic!

Picking up a car the following year in Mallorca was an altogether different experience. A few foreign assignments in the intervening year had given me a little more confidence about driving on the other side of the road as well as learning the pitfalls of hiring a vehicle abroad, such as making sure that all the mechanical parts were where they were supposed to be. The ghastly denouement of the previous year's trip to the Costas was the sight of us sitting by the road choking on an ugly cloud of black smoke pouring from the engine which had lost all its oil because the rocker-box cap was missing. This time the hire car official was left tapping his fingers in frustration as I gave the vehicle an MOT before signing any paperwork. The car's arrival half-way through the holiday had been timed perfectly. Over the previous few days I had been re-acquainting myself with the songs of Serin and Sardinian Warbler that rang out over the hotel gardens as well as trying to get to grips with the various plumage features of the Audouin's Gulls loafing on the beach. I was ready to head for some of the tantalising hotspots that I had read about longingly in Watkinson's guide more than a decade before and which had become some of the best-known places on the globetrotting birder's itinerary.

One bird, arguably the species I wanted to see more than any other bird on Earth, had already winged its way not just on to my list but into my life, too. To say I craved Eleonora's Falcon was an understatement. Missing this most dazzling of predators during our honeymoon, even when we dedicated a whole day to visiting its most famous hunting grounds on the rocky tip of Formentor, had been down to horrendous October weather rather than any preoccupation with nuptials. Missing it again on Crete, where it only breeds on the most remote and inaccessible offshore islands could be taken on the chin. In between, I had failed to see the falcon on our first holiday abroad with the children. That had been an abject failing of my identification skills. Now the time was right. We had just witnessed the passing of the summer solstice and the falcons were arriving in the western Mediterranean en masse from their wintering grounds on Madagascar to take advantage of the autumn songbird harvest. I was also better read. The phantom shapes of these ethereal birds had already proved tantalising, passing overhead at dusk as the family ate al fresco in the hotel grounds.

By the third night I was ready. Dinner was delayed for a rather unusual aperitif. Climbing to the hotel roof before the sun vanished over the western horizon, I set up my scope and waited. Cicadas chirped. Nightingale song reached a crescendo. Below, tourists in their evening finery chinked glasses and jangled cutlery. The sky darkened. *Whishhh*... A black rapier cut through the sky, vanishing before I could bring my binoculars up to my eyes. Shooosh! Another ghostly silhouette shot by and vanished over the stone pines that carpeted the horizon. My eyes squeezed every last drop of light from dusk's grip. And then...

My log takes up the story:

At last! Eleonora's Falcon does exist. To think I could have ever confused this most elegant and graceful of falcons with Peregrine. It is like comparing Mike Tyson with a prima ballerina. The Peregrine is a street-fighting bruiser, all power and punch – Eleonora's, as its name implies, is a true princess of the skies, not so much flying but holding court on the wing. Watching them tonight has been one of my most exciting birding experiences. The light was poor, but even in the gloom it was easy to pick out the main ID features, albeit that many of the birds were wholly dark-phase types. And when I say many, I mean many! At one stage, I counted 42 individuals weaving and careening over the large lake (S'Estany Gran) opposite the hotel. I guess they are hunting dragonflies – it's still too early for any autumn migrants – but they are far more refined in their technique: not the smash-and-grab style of a Hobby but more like sirens, hypnotising their unfortunate victims with the sheer brilliance of their flight before snatching them with deadly talons.

Nature's spectacular show lasted less than half an hour before night took hold and the bright lights of a bustling holiday resort filled the sky with a sickly orange glow. I was ecstatic, so much so that talking about it over dinner whetted the appetites of a few fellow guests who asked to see the falcons at play. The next evening, the hotel management opened the roof and a small gathering of British tourists stood in awe watching the falcons putting on their equivalent of a fireworks display. By the end of our stay, the Eleonora's Falcon aerial spectacular had become something of an international event, with families from Germany, Sweden, the Netherlands and Denmark regularly clambering to the roof to enjoy a pre-dinner appetiser.

Besides enthusing about the beauty of the falcons, one other event dominated conversation among the international community: the World Cup. In 24 hours Bobby Robson's Three Lions would be meeting the might of West Germany, old rivals that had last battled for football's greatest prize almost 20 years ago to the day. I had witnessed the heartbreak of Germany's 3–2 victory in Mexico through schoolboy tears; Italia 1990, I told myself, would be a time for revenge. There would be time for some pre-match birding, too.

Back home, the tabloids were carrying 'England Expects' banner headlines; in Turin, a raggle-taggle army of football fans was assembling in the city's ornate Piazza Castello for the most important football match for two decades. They sung 'Nessun Dorma' as their St George's flags flapped in the cool morning breeze sweeping down from the distant Alps. The irony of Puccini's aria may have been lost on some. Few had slept. I had only slept lightly, too. If I had not been dreaming about birds, they were certainly the first thing on my mind as the travel alarm squeaked into life. Today was going to be a birding adventure unlike any I had experienced before. We would be heading up into the Tramuntana Mountains, Mallorca's highest range and a destination that had teased and eluded me since I first picked up a copy of Eddie Watkinson's guide more than a decade earlier and read about the legendary Cuber Reservoir.

Having played the dutiful dad, willingly submitting myself to being buried up to my neck in sand, ducked in the sea, providing a non-stop beach waiter service and building more castles than the Dukes of Northumberland, this was to be my day. The children looked forlorn as I clipped them into their car seats with a story that we were visiting the 'seaside in the mountains' and repeatedly saying, 'Okay, take me to Cuber' as if I was a revolutionary Marxist plane hijacker. My humour was lost on the kids who remained silent and passive for all of 10 minutes before uttering the words every motoring father dreads: 'Are we there yet?'

Like distance posts, the same four words punctuated our journey as we left Alcudia, pottered along Mallorca's main central highway, skirted past the small, forgettable town of Inca and then began the long climb out of the lowlands into the island's mountainous spine. Every game of I-spy, every verse of 'wheels on the bus', was punctuated with the same hoary question and elicited the same response of 'not far now'. Hairpins were navigated and packed coaches overtaken; bushes were sought out for comfort stops and there was even time to watch a Hoopoe parading on the side of the road, serenaded, if that's the right word, by the mournful, staccato notes of a Cirl Bunting.

Eventually we arrived in mountain country. High peaks and rocky edifices crowded around us, promising good birds, but I dared not be distracted by the flash of raptor wings on a route where one error of judgement could be catastrophic. A crumpled and burnt out car at the bottom of one ravine helped keep my focus. Bumpy roads continued to coil around the limestone mountainsides like a writhing constrictor. In the buffeted backseats, the children had fallen ominously silent. Call it birder's instinct, but I could sense we were near journey's end. Puig Mayor, Mallorca's highest peak, shrugged off her misty morning shroud and looked down upon a sweeping, turquoise plateau twinkling in the sunlight – Cuber Reservoir. This remote and desolate spot was Eddie Watkinson's birding Shangri-La, a mere two hours' drive from tourist Gomorrah, but a place where one of Europe's rarest birds kept a powerful talon-hold on survival.

Adrenalin took over. I was out of the car and fumbling with unwieldy tripod legs before the engine had stopped turning over, my eyes constantly scanning the scenery for anything that resembled a bird shape. Scratchy birdsong resonated in the distance. Anne was still buried in the car, rousing the girls. Then a black shape, as vast as any bird form I had ever seen, glided overhead, silently and effortlessly eclipsing the sun and throwing a shadow over the rocky ground.

'Black Vulture!' I screamed as if I was standing amid a 1,000-strong twitch and had relocated some elusive rarity.

'Anne, Anne... Up there! Black Vulture!'

There was no response. I did not dare take my binoculars away from the vulture as it powered its mighty pinions to gain elevation. I guessed from the silence that Anne was spellbound by the majesty of Europe's most impressive raptor. Then, the commotion began. Welling travel sickness in the children erupted spectacularly. Charlotte projectile-vomited, and Anne emerged from the bowels of the car looking like she had been confronted by an irate Fulmar. She smelled like it, too. Emily had also received a coating, causing her to burst into tears and then start vomiting in synchronicity. It was a miracle I heard the Tawny Pipit as it launched into its mellifluous song, fluttering butterfly-like over the rocky reservoir foreshore. As soon as the pipit landed and disappeared from sight, I homed in like a locked-on missile. Anne was far from impressed.

'I need help,' she pleaded.

'I need Tawny Pipit. It's a new one!' I responded.

'You are heading for trouble,' came Anne's stern reply.

'I'm heading over there....'

By the time I returned from securing a framed scope view of the biscuit-toned pipit with its subtle head markings and jaunty carriage, Anne had cleaned up the children with wet wipes and was congratulating herself on packing them a change of clothing. There was no such luxury for her. Never underestimate the resoluteness of a woman. Because we were in such a remote spot, Anne decided to strip down and rinse her frock and undies with bottled water.

Even the writers of the *Carry On* films could not have dreamed up the next scene. The very moment Anne was peeling off her knickers, a coach pulled up, spilling its noisy company of tourists with the precision of a paratroop exercise. The crazy mullet haircuts, sports clothing and loud voices meant only one thing: Germans. Even to a nation that gave the world the philosophy of naturism, the sight of a young woman as naked as nature intended on the banks of a mountain reservoir must have seemed strange. At the very moment that 50 pairs of eyes focussed on Anne, who was hurriedly crossing her hands to hide her modesty, another bird took to the air. This time it was a Spectacled Warbler, delivering its exhilarating song as if it were waving a Sixties football rattle. I took off my Tottenham Hotspur shirt and threw it to Anne to save her blushes and then turned round and tried to relocate the skulking warbler, explaining in somewhat irritated terms that it was another new bird for me.

The Germans continued to gawp before bursting into a familiar song whose lyrics transcend the lingua franca of football fans. Anne's modesty forbids me from saying any more. (If a clue is needed, it was sung to the tune of 'Bread of Heaven' and has a line about getting something out for the lads).

That night, Gazza cried and England lost. The curse of the penalty shoot-out robbed Bobby Robson's team of a place in the World Cup Final. Mallorca, an island Germany once offered to lease from Spain because of the high number of its tourists taking their hard-earned Deutschmarks overseas, rocked to a Teutonic beat. The pilsner flowed and the songs – one of which I had heard earlier that day – rang out. Alcudia was no place to be if you were English. Streets were awash with black, red and gold. A lattice work of fingers had covered my eyes for most of the game and I turned my back for its nerve-wracking finale, listening to the groans of the small band of Englishmen squeezed into a sports bar as our penalty-takers came up to the mark – and failed. Defeat's bitter taste dried my mouth and brought back schoolboy memories of Sir Alf Ramsey's team crashing out to Franz Beckenbauer and Gerd Muller in 1970. I had cried that day, but this time there was something to fill me with a sense of well-being. Heading back to the hotel, a young, wild-eyed German, drunk on the heady brew of victory and a half dozen bottles of lager, staggered towards me, my sobriety obviously singling me out as an Englishman to be ridiculed. With a slur, he muttered something which could be loosely translated as 'the war is over for you, Englander'.

I smiled a stoic smile and thought to myself, 'Okay, you won the match, but did you see Black Vulture, Tawny Pipit and Spectacled Warbler today?'

Two Countries Divided by a Single Language

California, 1991

Google Earth is a wonderful 21st-century resource for wannabe globetrotters but there is nothing like staring down from 40,000 feet to the incredible tableau that is the surface of planet Earth. Perhaps it was the tedium of the in-flight film, or the few remaining glaciology factoids still pin-balling around my brain from my A-level days, but I marvelled at what was being unfurled five miles below for hour-after-hour of my first trans-Atlantic flight. It only added to the bubbling excitement of a plum foreign assignment.

As a newly appointed news editor on the *Daily Star* I had somehow wangled the 'freebie of the year' – the chance to write a feature on the razzamatazz tourist attractions that might lure British families to swap the Spanish Costas for the sunshine coast of

Southern California. Mickey Mouse, Beverly Hills, ET, Universal Studios and hamburger culture beckoned with open arms. In truth, I was looking forward more to seeing my first American birds.

If you have never spent hours playing I-spy with Google Earth, or if you have made the gruelling 8,000-mile flight from London Heathrow to Los Angeles LAX but have neglected to peer out the cabin windows, then what you have missed is a chance to gaze upon some of the most desolate but fascinating panoramas produced by nature's forces. Damning evidence of mankind's insatiable desire to apply concrete to the ground like greasepaint is also there to behold. Looking down at the seemingly endless Canadian tundra with its permafrost topography of pingos – frozen earth mounds that can rise 200 feet – and the splattering of countless kettle lakes, I imagined the birds below: waders in breeding finery to match the rusty hues of the stunted vegetation, marauding skuas, wild geese and mighty Gyr Falcons, each playing out its annual survival game under an Arctic summer sun that never sets.

Ice-flecked, treeless wastes eventually gave way to the Midwest's 'badlands', appearing from afar as vast a pizza topping or a bad case of teenage acne. This is the arid, inhospitable land the Lakota Sioux called *Makhósica*, a place of uncompromising beauty. Red rock canyons and ravines, rain-carved gullies and wind-shaped hoodoos – tall, chimney like stacks of soft rock – have been the backdrop to dramatic episodes in America's young history as well as countless cowboy films. General George Armstrong Custer died with his boots on here and Charles Stackweather also went on his murderous rampage, a killing spree made all the more infamous by *Badlands*, the eponymous Seventies film starring Martin Sheen. Looking down at the long straight roads that dissect the Dakotas, Wyoming and Montana like cheese wire, I conjured up images of Red-tailed Hawks huddled on fence posts or mewing on the wing as terrified Prairie Dogs scurried to the safety of their dugouts.

Two incredible landscapes successfully navigated, the final stage of the flight was over arguably some of the most dangerous habitat anywhere on Earth – greater Los Angeles. Flying over the sprawl of unprepossessing, single-storey properties that stretched from the San Gabriel Mountains to the shoreline of the Pacific took an age. One could only imagine what stories were being played out in a city that personifies the American dream, with its opulent Bel Air mansions and Beverly Hills excess, but also plays witness to the spectres of drug-taking, gang warfare and First World poverty. Within an hour, I would be trying to survive in this ultimate urban jungle.

American border control officers take no prisoners. Glum faces and curt questions put new arrivals on edge. No smiley welcome or high-five greeted me as I queued in the arrivals lounge at LAX clutching my pristine passport with its shiny new 'I visa', the United States' entry requirement for official foreign correspondents. I was walking in the footsteps of Pilger and Whicker. The customs officer made me feel like Osama bin Laden. Even in the summer of 1991, a whole decade before the events of 9/11, America's hair-trigger approach to foreign nationals meant anyone stepping on its hallowed soil was open to suspicion. My bouncy attempts at geniality were ignored, apart from a terse question about the reason for my trip.

'I've come to see Mickey Mouse,' I said, trying to lighten the mood. 'Do you know him?'

There was no response but this time I could have sworn the stoic immigration officer's hand brushed a right hip decorated with a holstered Smith and Wesson .38 before handing me back my disingenuously stamped passport. 'Have a nice day,' I said with lashings of sarcasm. A grunt was volleyed back. Irony, I was to learn all too soon, is not part of the American psyche.

Navigating Surlyville, USA, seemed to have taken as long as passing over Canada's vast icy wildernesses. At least the next task would be straightforward, I told myself, as I passed a credit card and driving licence to the car hire clerk who ushered me to the awaiting sports coupe with lots of obsequious jibber-jabber. America's extremes were already beginning to grate.

Finding my hotel on Wilshire Boulevard, a 20-minute drive from the airport, was supposed to be a cinch. A steak, beer and a good night's sleep beckoned, then four full days to experience some good ol' West Coast hospitality in one of the Lower 48's 'birdiest' states. Since I had been given my brief to write a travel piece about the sights, sounds and flesh-pots of the City of the Angels, I had spent almost every free hour picking out its best birding locations and had worked out an itinerary so that I could tick off Disneyland, Rodeo Drive, Venice Beach and Malibu as well as putting my brand new National Geographic *Field Guide to the Birds of North America* to good use. The Ford Probe's 2.2 turbo engine roared into life, the seat belt automatically crossed my chest and that it was it. Nothing. I had taken hire of an automatic drive. I may as well have been piloting the Space Shuttle. The Hispanic car park attendant laughed out loud.

'You only have manual shifts in England?' He asked with the same incredulity as if I told him we still joust and live in castles. His driving lesson lasted all of five minutes and he doubled it up with instructions on how to get out of the airport hinterland and into LA proper without having to resort to the table mat-sized map that came with the car keys.

Two hours later I was still driving. Green road signs pointing to Pasadena and Long Beach, Anaheim and Santa Monica came and went. The staccato words of James Ellroy, the brilliant nihilistic author of America's bête noir crime novels, stabbed home. LA was the City of Angels, but had no soul. Each street was a pastiche of American life: big, brusque, but charmless. Radio Shacks flashed by. McDonalds loomed and disappeared. Cadillacs and sports utilities muscled up threateningly, windows blacked out and, I convinced myself, full of gangstas lurking behind the darkened glass with Mac-10 'spray and pray' machine pistols. Everywhere there were signs of the Bloods and Crips, the streets' most notorious gangs, staking claim on the city with rock art graffiti homages to fallen comrades scrawled on billboards and every open wall space. I had become hopelessly lost.

At one street corner, I foolishly asked the way from a gathering of young men dressed in basketball vests to accentuate bodies tattooed like road maps. Bad move. The sense of pure hate was palpable. Hand signs in the shape of guns reinforced my decision to get back in the car and head into the night. Foot down, another hour passed. More place names flashed by – Compton, Inglewood, Firestone – inner city ghettoes that, within a year, were to become synonymous with street riots and civil disturbance when Rodney King's racially motivated beating by LA's finest became global news.

Apart from the gangs, the sidewalks were ominously empty. Only a growing sense of foreboding kept my eyes open and my mind alert; apart from the drip, drip of fright-induced adrenalin I was running on empty. Seductive thoughts of pulling over and sleeping in some back alley began making sense. Flashing red lights snapped me back to reality. Black-and-white cars blocked the road. Uniformed figures were circled around a beaten up saloon. Torches flashed in the dark. My first instinct was to get out of the car and ask for help. Before I had both feet on the road, a voice boomed out from the gloom.

'Get back in the car!'

'But I'm lost. Do you know the way to Wilshire Boulevard?' I whimpered.

'Get back in the car. Now!'

'But I'm English,' I said, trying to add a hint of public school clipped vowels to an accent honed in a state-run comprehensive.

'I am warning you, Sir. Get back in the car. This is your last chance.' I was oblivious to the tension I was adding to an already fraught situation. Only when I saw the bullet-proof vests emblazoned with word SWAT was it obvious I had stumbled into an everyday story of gangstas and cops on the mean streets of the Big Orange. Two figures lay supine on the ground, their hands hogtied behind them, carbines pointing at their heads.

'Sir, I am telling you now...'

I moved cautiously back behind the steering wheel, nodding my head compliantly, hands held up in surrender.

Seconds later a torch beam caught me full in the eyes. The car door opened.

'You almost got yourself shot, Sir.' I was shaking too much to speak. 'What's your problem?' The question was stark, lacking compassion.

In one sentence I spurted out my life story, adding every detail of the nightmare search for my hotel on Wilshire Avenue for good measure. Minutes later, I was pulling into a car park, courtesy of an LAPD escort. The five-mile drive from LAX to the heart of the city had taken almost four hours. I was exhausted and half-traumatised but one thing kept me focussed. Tomorrow I was going birding.

The soft cry of a dove woke me while it was still dark. 'Who are you...you...you?' It seemed to be saying in mournful tones. I was still too tired, too disorientated, to know the answer. The allure of a soft bed had me turning my back to the window and its single bird dawn chorus. More calls, this time louder, more strident. Birding instincts took over. A sleepy mind began deducing what species was being so noisy. Woodpigeon, Collared, Stock and Turtle Doves were eliminated. Then it dawned: a new day in the New World. I had just connected with my first American bird, a yard bird, a trash bird for many Stateside birders, a bird so numerous that an estimated 70 million are shot by hunters every year, but a new tick, all the same.

That wonderful realisation that I was going birding, not in just a new country but in a new continent, erased all fatigue.

Ever since I had been given my American briefing by the Travel Editor I had longed for this moment. I only wished I had put as much effort into planning my journey from the airport as I had spent poring over maps and researching the adventure I was about to embark upon. Midsummer's Day, the first wafts of sunlight lightening the sky: time to hit the road.

An hour later, I was parked up in a quiet cul-de-sac somewhere in Greater Los Angeles not knowing where I was or where to go next. One of southern California's notorious summer sea mists had cloaked the city in a heavy haze, mixing with the infamous pollution for good measure to make it extra opaque. My internal compass had gone haywire. I had no idea which way was north. At the time I had expected to hit the coast road, I was entangled in a road system that made the Gordian Knot look like a tied shoelace. In a state of panic, I found myself exiting to some anonymous neighbourhood for sanctuary from the morning rush hour.

I was lost. I needed help. But I was in America. Joggers brushed me aside. Dog-walkers cocooned in Walkman oblivion ignored my pleas. When I attempted to wave down a car, the driver sped off, twisting his index finger against his temple to press home his views of my lunacy. I yearned for home. I was even pondering going back to the airport and catching the first flight back to the UK when a flash of blue caught my eye. Across the road, a cocky, upright bird was patrolling the sidewalk with the jaunty step of a policeman from an old Laurel and Hardy film. He walked one way and then promptly spun around to step out in the opposite direction, before nonchalantly marching off the kerb to peck at some long-flattened roadkill. I reached for my binoculars.

The bird was a beautiful combination of cobalt blue crown, wings and tail, with a white bib and black mask. I reached for my

National Geographic, with a good idea of its identity. If it was jay-walking it must be a jay ... but which one? Page 300 yielded the answer – a Scrub Jay of the Pacific race. As I watched it continue its morning promenade, the first glint of sunshine broke through the haze. The bird twisted its head, closed both eyes and soaked up the first warm rays of the day. As the creature went into what could only be described as a trance, I felt not only empathy for its joie de vivre but also an overwhelming desire to see more, hear more and enjoy more American birds. The sun's position also helped me realise that I had spent an hour driving eastwards when I should have been heading west. It was time to find the most famous road in America: Route 66.

As anyone who has got their kicks on this 2,000 mile slab of concrete will tell you, journey's end is on Hollywood's famous Sunset Boulevard as it snakes down through Santa Monica to the shimmering Pacific. A road sign nailed proudly to a Beverly Hills utility mast was emblazoned with the words 'The Mother Road – Route 66'. Finally, I was well on course for the next leg of my quest: to find California's Highway One, the iconic coastal road which connects Los Angeles with San Fransisco.

The Pacific Coast Highway has seen more filmed car chases than any other road in cinema history. H1 oozes speed as it breaks out of urban sprawl and skirts the chaparral-covered hillsides that overlook the ocean, the bends and twists adding to the excitement of the drive. My foot caressed the accelerator and the turbo kicked in. I twiddled the radio tuner to find a motoring anthem for the long drive north. U2's 'With or Without You' throbbed through the sound system. Gulls whizzed by but I was on a mission. No time to bird, just yet. An all-American breakfast beckoned. Overhead a dark shape caught my eye – a raptor. The gulls could wait, but my first bird of prey deserved respect. Before I could stop, a figure stepped out into the road ahead. The tan-coloured uniform and park ranger-style Stetson meant only one thing: I was being busted by the CHiPs, the Californian Highway Patrol.

The Patrolman's Raybans were so shiny I could see my flustered reflection fidgeting nervously. He had clocked me at 50 mph in a 40 mph zone and I had some explaining to do. Fast. He looked mean and every time he moved his right hand, it drew attention to the wooden handle of his .38 revolver. I gulped.

'I'm, er, English...' It sounded the perfect gambit. Surely there was some sort of Constitutional immunity from speeding fines for the British abroad.

'I thought the speed signs were in kilometres...' I continued, speaking with the superior accent of an English toff. The cop must have come from Revolutionary stock. He looked dour. I tried a little Bob Hoskins. 'Er, sorry, mate. First time in the US of A, you know. Your roads over 'ere are more like our motorways back 'ome,' I explained, giving him a chirpy, Cockney smile.

'Surprising you could see the speed signs – you were driving on the other side of the road...' I waited for the Smokey to finish his sentence with the regulation 'Sir'. It never came.

The patrolman's chiselled features remained emotionless and seemed to merge with the razor sharp creases of his uniform as if they were all part of one mechanism. I kept thinking of Robocop. 'Um, sorry, officer,' I stammered. 'Er, I mean, Sir. I am very sorry – it's my first visit to your great country.'

I proffered my virgin passport with its solitary red US Immigration stamp, the only mark among an expanse of blank pages. He also wanted my driving documents.

'This is a licence?' His robotic voice creaked with incredulity as he clasped the decaying document between thumb and index finger as if it was a soiled diaper. The licence had seen better days and although it was dog-eared and heavily stained at least it was 'clean' in the motoring sense.

'This is an *English* driving licence?' He repeated with even more incredulity, looking me up and down and muttering something about poor old Limeys and the Third World.

'You're our most important ally and you're using toilet napkins for licences. Gee. God help America.'

The Raybans came off and the stony facade turned to one of pity.

'Drive safely. And preferably on the right side of the road,' was his passing shot as he marched towards his gleaming patrol car, shaking his head. Who said the Americans had no sense of irony?

I looked up. The Turkey Vulture that had caused my predicament was circling on dihedral wings. It sensed blood. I was hungry, too.

As a recent convert to the world of vegetarianism, my following admission is likely to get me excommunicated from the brotherhood of non-meat eaters. That first breakfast driving north to Ventura is a meal that I can still taste and relish to this day.

'Two sausage egg McMuffins, bacon on the side, hash browns, hotcakes, coffee and a box of cookies coming straight up,' said the pretty counter clerk with a picture perfect smile, teeth lined up like the front guard of a gridiron team.

'Have a nice day,' she soothed, as sickly as a five-dollar shake.

'Thank you,' I responded instinctively.

'You're welcome, Sir,' she retaliated, desperate to have the final say.

This programmed, insincere dialogue was to become an increasingly infuriating feature of visits to fast-food outlets over the following days. Show your gratitude and Americans always have to go one better. Try begging for help when you're lost and you may as well be a leper. Hand over a few crusty Greenbacks and you're treated like a Tinsel Town A-lister. That said, the breakfast tasted great – and the following course was good, too. Refuelled, coffee-to-go in one hand, Leicas draped around my neck, I fixed my drawtube

Optolyth scope to the tripod, slipped the National Geographic guide between my belt and the small of my back and got working.

The McDonalds restaurant proved a perfect place to begin my Great American Birding Adventure. Everything was new. Western and Ring-billed Gulls patrolled overhead on the lookout for easy meals; House Finches sang from nearby television aerials; American Crows loitered with intent; Brewer's Blackbirds patrolled the parking lot like traffic attendants in uniform and a flock of Bushtits bickered their way through a tangle of bougainvillea. Across the highway, a swirl of flying shapes above the Pacific Ocean beckoned. One quick dash across the perilous road and I was looking out at a seabird spectacular as frantic as anything I had ever seen. Brown Pelicans were on dive-bombing missions, seemingly guarded by flocks of Forster's Terns acting as fighter cover. The fleeting wings of countless gulls in countless plumage permutations created a kind of bird blindness. I needed to focus on one thing. A wader caught my eye: medium size, medium length bill and medium legs, this poor, nondescript bird looked as if it had been designed by a committee. There was nothing distinctive about it. I wracked my brain ... far too big for a Calidrid sandpiper, too bulky for a *Tringa*. I began jotting notes, but found little to recommend it. Then it took off with an explosion of black-and-white wings and a loud call of its name. A Willet!

Out at sea, a raft of grebes bobbed aimlessly, necks held aloft like ballerinas and long, stiletto-like bills bestowing a serpent-like demeanour. I had seen Western Grebes performing their intricate mating dances on wildlife documentaries, and although the breeding rituals had long ended, it never diminished my excitement watching these delicate creatures at ease among the breaking rollers. The beach was not only a hive of bird activity. This was Malibu, beach resort nonpareil. Joggers and surfers, body-builders and sun-lovers practised their arts on its fine sands. At the time, *Baywatch* and the incredible contours of Pamela Anderson were only just beginning to impact on the Saturday evening meal-time arrangements of millions of British families – well, the men – but for birdwatchers the show regularly served up titillating views of arguably the world's most beautiful gull. As Pammy paraded in her super-tight swimsuit, it was the hope of catching sight of the scarlet bill of Heermann's Gull that made the show compulsive viewing in many a birder's household. Now I was looking at one in the flesh. An adult bird in its multitude of grey tones was picking at flotsam, the contrast between its snowy head and blood-stained bill discernible at 200 paces. In the scope, it was more eye-catching than any bikini-clad lovely.

'What ya doing?' A beach dude loaded up with McDonald's carry-outs broke the spell.

'I'm birding!' I said, all-American style.

'Sure, bet, Dude!' He responded. 'With all those babes about...'

It was time to go. The sight of an eccentric British tourist with lilywhite legs sticking out of football shorts spying at a beach laden with scantily clad lovelies was beginning to draw attention. I needed to find somewhere to birdwatch in solitude. My Ventura County road map was about to be put to good use.

American history was built on the greatness of its rivers. The mighty Mississippi, the wide Missouri, the Ohio, Mohawk, Colorado, Rio Grande... From New York's Hudson in the east to the Yukon carving its way across Arctic Alaska, men have used and abused the Continent's river systems to push back the frontiers, tame the landscape and create the American dream. Compared to the great waterways gouging mountains and prairies, the little Santa Clara is nothing more than a muddy stream that runs towards the sea a few miles south of Ventura. The distance from its headwaters high on the northern slopes of the San Gabriel to its gaping mouth on the Pacific is little more than 100 miles and the last few miles of its meandering journey are so sluggish that it regularly fails to make ocean fall. Instead of a gaping river mouth the slow trickle produces a wide, stagnating lagoon.

These tranquil, tepid waters were my target as I headed away from Los Angeles, the Pacific to my left, the Boney Mountain State Wilderness to my right. The 30-mile journey was hardly an epic road trip, but every few minutes there was a reason to stop, to take in the grandeur or enjoy new birds. A Hooded Oriole, golden plumage glistening as it sang from a telegraph wire, was a welcome introduction to this 24-carat group of American specialities. Five miles on, a striking Red-shouldered Hawk, fiery epaulettes merging to form a brilliant orange breast band, almost stayed perched long enough for me to take a photograph before it powered off on its heavily patterned wings.

While Highway One continued to weave north towards Santa Barbara, the Big Sur and beyond, it was time for me to hit smalltownsville with its double-garaged, wooden houses that always come with basketball hoops, fluttering Stars and Stripes and large sports utilities parked on the driveway. Location One on my five-day itinerary was the McGrath State Park, named in honour of a wealthy property-owning dynasty from the days of the 19th-century Californian land grab, and which overlooked the Santa Clara River. Months must have passed since the river had last reached the ocean and now the water was shallow, algae-laden and smelly. This did not deter the birds.

Teeming flocks of waders infested the shallows and ducks, gulls and herons covered the deeper areas. I scanned this vibrant vista with still-vivid memories of stepping into one of Minsmere's Scrape hides as a child some 20 years before. On that day I had seen my first Avocets, Black-tailed Godwits, Spotted Redshanks and Little Terns. Looking out from the parking lot, I could see my birds' long-lost American cousins. American Avocets tip-toed with upturned bills, but unlike the boys back home these dandies had rusty, sun-blushed heads. The same cinnamon-tones adorned another large wader using its more subtly up-curved bill to probe the gooey margins. Its shape reminded me of a 'Barwit' (Bar-tailed Godwit), and flicking through the field guide soon had me nodding at the illustration of the tortoiseshell-patterned Marbled Godwit.

I could not wait to get down to the water's edge to enjoy the shorebird spectacular at close quarters. Suddenly, something shot past my face, too fast, too bulky to be an insect but surely too small for a bird. The buzzing ball of energy whizzed back, this time stalling mid-flight as if to eye me before continuing with its flight plan. The freeze frame was enough to see it was a hummingbird – my first ever – but which one? The field guide offered lots of confusing alternatives and I cursed my observational skills for not taking in more field marks. In an instant, the bird returned. With a tongue almost the same length as its entire body, it savoured a flower at eye level. A twist of its head caught the light perfectly and its dowdy head pattern suddenly exploded into a shock of iridescent red as bright and dazzling as the Black Prince's 170-carat ruby in the Crown Jewels. A flurry of page-turning revealed the bird I was looking at had its own regal antecedents. Anna's Hummingbird, the West Coast's commonest hummer, is named in honour of Anna D'Essling, the wife of Prince Victor, a 19th-century French bird collector.

Renowned birder Mark Cocker describes the mood as 'full bonus', the moment the ornithological gods smile down and offer their gifts to us mere mortals. Everywhere I turned I was seeing new birds. Illustrations of American Goldfinches, Bullock's Oriole and Spotted Towhee were jumping off the pages of the field guide and morphing into living, breathing entities. Addictive stuff and I needed more fixes. I took off my trainers, knotted the laces, draped them over my shoulder and began wading into the warm, rank waters of the Santa Clara, focussed on one small sand bar that looked like a rotting corpse being picked to the bone by flesh-hungry flies. For flies, read 'peeps' – America's confusing, no, confounding, group of Calidrid sandpipers. This small group of shorebirds, close relatives of Europe's Little and Temminck's Stints, were my number one target birds. The late, great Peter Grant had put me on their trail with a 1984 British Birds paper on these fascinating, sparrow-size waders, made all the more alluring by Lars Jonsson's artwork. Semipalmated, Western and Least Sandpipers are rare wanderers to our shores and even when they do arrive their feather tracts, bare parts and behavioural traits require forensic analysis to secure positive identifications and the confidence to submit a report to the so-called 'Rare Men' – the British Birds Rarities Committee. Now I was looking at all three species as they scurried like clockwork mice, picking morsels from the simmering invertebrate soup.

The peeps – the etymology of the word is misted by time but it is believed to derive from either their trill calls or an old word for young chickens – were oblivious to the human form in their midst and, indeed, were so confiding they were picking at food at my feet. All were in summer plumage and were either still en route to Canadian nesting grounds or had lost the all-powerful sexual urge to head to the top of the world and find a mate. Whatever the reason for remaining at a latitudinal equivalent of northern Morocco, the peeps provided an identification masterclass.

Peep identification has been discussed over hundreds of pages of esoteric ornithological literature and still perplexes records committees to this day, but watching these tiny sprites tippy-tapping at such close range it was soon easy to identify them as much by their shape, size and structure as it was their plumage details. In short, the Leasts were tiny, tortoiseshell-patterned with greenish legs and a fine, decurved bill. Westerns, by contrast, were larger, 'Dunlin-like', with a longer down-curved bill, black legs and a rufous tinge to their crown, ear coverts and scapulars. The only Semipalmated present was much duller than the Westerns and had a shorter, blunter bill. 'Eureka, I've cracked it!' I convinced myself.

Now was time to turn my attention to the dowitchers, which were far less confiding. As I raised my binoculars, I noticed a single-file crocodile of a half-dozen or so people wading towards me. I had not heard them above the clamour of screaming Least and Forster's Terns and the squabbling Black-necked Stilts. The binoculars, baseball caps and scopes marked them out as birders.

'What ya got, boy?' boomed a voice as Southern as grits and red-eye gravy and without a hint of decorum. The speaker had a complexion as rough as rattlesnake skin and was wearing a baseball cap glistening with American bird club badges. I took him to be the group leader.

'Stints, er, I mean peeps, thousands of them.' I replied.

'Oh, I don't do peeps, they're bewildering little critters,' one of the group's female members piped up. She was a good ten years older than the leader and as wide as she was tall. Her T-shirt was emblazoned with two cutesy bluebirds and the slogan 'I Love Birds'. The old dear's binoculars had most probably come from a nickel and dime shop.

I went into expert mode.

'They're not so difficult when you get a good view. Take Western Sandpiper, for instance. You can tell it by its jizz.'

A round of chesty guffaws and cries of 'Oh, my God!' broke out. One of the women looked as if she was about to faint. She waved her hand in front of her face like a fan. The atmosphere changed as if I had told a risqué joke to a Women's Institute meeting. Several of the women, who looked like they had walked off the set of *The Waltons*, wandered off muttering about the manners of 'so-called English gentlemen'. I was flummoxed and the leader looked nonplussed, too. Before I could speak he hurried away, calling to the women who were now wading back the way they came. As he tried to placate them, he turned round signalling me to stay put. Five minutes later, he returned alone.

'Sorry about that,' I apologised. 'Was it something I said?

'Gee, boy,' the drawl came straight out of the Southern boondocks. 'I know you Brit birders know their stuff, but that sure takes some beatin'.'

He stood scratching his day-old stubble.

'What do you mean?' I replied, even more mystified.

'The way you identified those li'l fellas.' He pointed to the peeps still pirouetting around our feet. 'That's smarter than Robert E. Lee on the day he graduated from West Point.'

I looked at him quizzically.

'Why, how d'ya goddamn tell 'em by their jizz?' His eyes bulged.

'It's just something we do in the UK,' I responded with open hands.

'Yeah, but how d'ya get the little *******'s semen in the first place?'

It suddenly dawned. On our side of the Atlantic, jizz was an acronym coined during the Second World War to help spotters identify enemy aircraft by General Impression, Size and Shape. The other side of the Pond it was a shortened form of jissum, slang that would never be heard in polite society and likely to get you run out of town in many places. George Bernard Shaw was right: we really are two countries divided by a single language.

East Side Story
New York, 1992

The following essay was my winning entry in the *BBC Wildlife* magazine's 2009 travel-writing competition and relates to the first incredible moments when a life-long dream became reality.

Sting or Gershwin: two cassettes, one Walkman – big choice. Clammy fingers fumble at the controls. A few reassuring clicks and clunks, and the chosen soundtrack roars into life. My Manhattan adventure is about to begin.

The opening 17-note clarinet trill of *Rhapsody in Blue* tingles the spine as I emerge from the dark bowels of Penn Station, only to have my senses mugged by the bright spring morning with its brilliant sunshine, speeding yellow taxis, screaming pretzel sellers and the hubbub typical of rush hour in midtown New York. There's no time to absorb the moment. A human tidal wave swirls past, anonymous faces angled downwards; none have the time to smile, no time to look up, no time to savour the explosion of sights, sounds and smells of a new working day in the world's most eclectic metropolis.

I have dreamed of visiting New York since childhood, inspired by the late Kenneth Allsopp's 1970s *World About Us* documentary on the city's wildlife, with its alligator-filled sewers and raccoon-ravaged trash cans. For a budding birdwatcher, the highlight was Central Park's colourful characters: crimson Northern Cardinals, raucous Blue Jays and the brightly marked wood-warblers that decorate the trees during the spring migration.

Countless note-filled exercise books and annotated maps were to become testament to the 20 years of planning. Now it is reality. I have choreographed my steps like a Broadway dance show: the trans-Atlantic flight, the sleepover in Newark, the dawn shuttle into Manhattan and the anthems to accompany my visit. Cue Gershwin…

Earphones adjusted, volume tweaked, I follow the human tsunami of suited office workers north along streets I had learned from afar. Yet two-dimensional maps have not prepared me for the 3-D reality. The giant, monolithic skyscrapers glisten like movie stars' teeth, while linear roads and avenues – their names etched into Big Apple folklore: 42nd Street, Fifth Avenue, Madison – slice through the blocks of 100-storey edifices like dental floss.

The 12 minutes 31 seconds it takes for *Rhapsody in Blue* to reach its crescendo is enough time for me to pass from concrete splurge to verdant oasis, though as I reach the tree-lined fringes of Central Park, the rat race takes on new forms. I dodge hurtling roller-skaters, obdurate joggers, manic dog-walkers and countless cyclists. There's a fugitive with a police posse, and even a detachment of boy scouts counting out a march, Green Beret-style. I now have one objective: to reach The Ramble, the most overgrown and sinister part of the park, but also its 'birdiest', to use the local vernacular. And the most dangerous.

As soon as I pass under leaf canopy, I am accosted by an elderly man. 'You birding?' he asks brusquely.

'Sure am,' I reply, trying to affect a Bronx accent.

The old man immediately rattles off an incredible tally of the warblers, thrushes, tanagers and vireos he has seen over the past hour. He senses I am a new kid on the block.

'Be careful in there,' he warns.

The Ramble was still a few years from being exorcised of its notorious reputation by New York's zero-tolerance laws.

'And if you see a dead body, leave well alone. The cops'll want to ask you too many questions. You may miss your flight back to England.'

I gulp.

The old man departs and soon I am lapping up The Ramble's treasures. The birds have names and colours that span the rainbow: Scarlet Tanagers, orange-hued Baltimore Orioles, Yellow Warblers, Black-throated Green and Black-throated Blue Warblers... I search longingly for an Indigo Bunting.

Then I notice it – a body. Sitting slouched against a tree root is a deathly pale cadaver dressed incongruously in a tuxedo. Two crimson spots glisten on the John Doe's dress shirt. A hit, a mafia hit! I panic. Before I can scream for help, the corpse comes to life.

'Shhh!' The ghoulish figure brings a finger to his lips and raises a pair of binoculars, nodding for me to look towards a distant point outside the park's boundary. I focus my own binoculars on the ornate façade of a swanky apartment block across from the park. It is decorated bizarrely with a bundle of twigs. Sitting atop is a splendid bird of prey – a Red-tailed Hawk.

'Ain't they great?' the cadaver speaks with a Don Corleone accent. I mumble in the affirmative.

'Just had to see the hawks before I go back on set,' the cadaver continues. 'Looks like I am going to have to reshoot that last scene. The director didn't like the way I died.'

We both turn our attentions to the Red-tailed Hawk as it opens its vast wings and takes flight.

Only in America, I muse, reaching for my Walkman. Sting's voice responds: 'I'm an Englishman in New York...'

New York had fascinated me from the moment my Dad told me that Superman's adopted home of Metropolis had been shaped on an incredible city of towering buildings that scraped the skies somewhere across a vast ocean. I was born and raised in London's bustling East End, and my early life was crammed with the colours and vibrancy that only urban life can produce. To think 3,000 miles to the west was a city, a heaving metropolis that was larger, more frenetic and influential, certainly more dangerous and on the edge than the capital of England, had me dreaming of one day walking in the footsteps of my favourite red-caped superhero. When intrepid BBC reporter Kenneth Allsop brought the city's vibrant wildlife, particularly its gaudy wood-warblers, into our front room one Sunday teatime the desire to visit New York became an obsession. It would be a calling that would take two decades to answer.

My feature on the star-spangled, razzmatazz holiday opportunities offered by Los Angeles, with its ET bicycle ride in Universal Studios and the colourful late night Electrical Parade along Disneyland's main thoroughfare, went down well with the travel editor. So much so that the following year, with the British Pound faring particularly well against the US dollar, I was asked if I would like to spend a couple of days in New York to write a shopping feature, comparing prices on Fifth Avenue and Broadway with those in Britain. 'Shopping? Me?' I asked an incredulous news editor.

Few things are total anathema in my life but the idea of trawling past glass-fronted stores looking for bargains and then having to queue at a till is up there with animal cruelty and watching Australian soap operas. My face must have revealed these inner aversions to department stores and fashion outlets.

'We can always get someone else,' the news editor told me as he outlined my mission: a 36-hour, shop-til-you-drop marathon checking out the prices on Main Street USA, listing everything from lingerie and cosmetics to the toys-for-boys electrical gadgetry that were years ahead of what was on offer on the British high street, and then writing a piece under the headline: Looking for a Bargain? Go West. Thoughts of pounding the streets of Manhattan with a notebook ticking off perfumes and make-up, ceramics, haberdashery and leather goods filled me with dread.

Then it clicked. All those years of planning fantasy visits to New York suddenly struck me like a Wall Street rush-hour commuter charge. Central Park, with its woods and tangled undergrowth, loomed large on my mental map of Manhattan. So did a chapter Bill Oddie had written for my book *Best Days with British Birds* in which he had waxed lyrically about a visit on 4 May 1965, when he had taken time out from a Broadway revue to bask in the glory of birds such as the 'Creeping Zebra Warbler' – his far more descriptive name for the monochromatic Black-and-white Warbler. Thoughts of one of these pied beauties shinning up a tree trunk brought me out in a dreamy smile. Years of planning make-believe journeys were about to become reality.

'You okay?' The news editor asked, dragging me back to my senses. I accepted the assignment with a purposeful nod of the head. 'We'll need your copy soonest. Don't hang around,' were my final instructions.

In truth, I never did have time to hang around. The cursory trip to the Ramble with its sprinkling of warblers, most too skittish to give satisfactory views, along with the Red-tailed Hawk and the meeting with the 'dead' thespian, were frustratingly small morsels to whet my appetite for East Coast American birds, hardly enough to satiate a life-long craving. Copy is king, as they say on national news desks, and the job had to come first. I needed to research and file before I left on the overnight 'red eye' to be back for work. Before leaving Manhattan for Newark Airport, I checked the news desk for any last minute instructions. There was one message: 'Speak to the Editor... urgently!' My stomach flipped.

'Ah, Stuart, while you're in New York could you get me some toothpaste?' The Editor rattled off the name of a particular brand I had not seen even though I had picked up, squeezed, shaken and rattled every commodity for sale from West 14th Street to the upper reaches of East 125th. I promised I would do my best. This meant failure was impossible.

After scouring Manhattan, I finally found the toothpaste in a little downtown drugs store and bought the entire stock. The next morning when I reached the customs gate at Heathrow Airport I was to rue that hasty decision.

For all my loathing of the retail industry, I did indulge in a few moments of MasterCard masochism: a hand-made colonial-style patchwork quilt for my wife, T-shirts, toys and a carrier bag full of candy for the girls, the recently unveiled Nintendo Game Boy for me and, best of all, a small library of bird books and teach-yourself song tapes. Weighed down like a bag lady or an unseasonal Santa, I opted for the red 'goods to declare' channel, thinking that even if I was expected to pay import duty it would provide a few additional facts and figures for my shopping article.

I plonked my wares onto the customs counter and began reeling off the purchases I had made during my mini-break. Out came a calculator and the steely-eyed customs officer, professional, polite but perhaps lacking a little bonhomie, began tapping furiously. I grimaced. Minutes passed and I was presented with a piece of a paper.

Fortunately, it was only the quilt that was creating a problem. The spirit of trans-Atlantic free trade had not permeated the fabrics industry and meant there was a hefty amount of duty to be paid for the privilege of turning our bedroom into something like *Bonanza*'s Ponderosa. Having paid for the quilt I was about to leave when the customs officer pointed to my travel holdall and indicated that he wanted to see its contents. Alongside my Peterson field guide, a pair of Leica Trinovids, a change of clothes and my shower bag there were enough tubes of toothpaste to keep the Osmonds lighting up the world with their diamond smiles for the next century. The officer broke into an almost equally radiant grin as if had struck gold.

'What have you here?' He asked, pondering whether he had just snared an international diamond smuggler or a drugs trafficker. 'Can you explain why would anyone want 20 tubes of toothpaste?'

I am sure I heard the sound of latex gloves being twanged in readiness in a back room. 'Erm...' Thoughts of intimate body searches left me a jabbering wreck. I took a deep breath but before I could begin explaining the story of my secret toothpaste assignment, the customs office began opening one of the tubes, gently squeezing the contents out into coiling white serpent. A tang of mint filled the stuffy room. Two or three squeezed tubes later and I was able to collect myself and explain why I had gone to New York and why I had become the planet's largest purchaser of a certain brand of toothpaste. The customs official laughed, kindly packed all the remaining tubes into my bag and bade me farewell.

'I don't think you'll be going back to New York in hurry,' he laughed.

'You must be joking,' I replied. 'I can't wait.'

There were birds to see...

Walking in the Shadow
of a Giant

Connecticut, 1995

Manhattan's skyline loomed large on the horizon like the battlements of some vast Gothic cathedral. The grand Empire State, the Art Deco splendour of the Chrysler Building with its ornate spire, the doomed Twin Towers of the World Trade Centre; each added their own distinctive outlines to a silhouette that had become indelibly printed in my mind's eye since that all too frenetic visit to New York three years before. As I crossed the East River and peered through the steel-wire, spider's web strands of the Brooklyn Bridge, those same pangs of excitement that struck me the moment I delved into the garish delights of Central Park's brilliant birds returned. This time, however, the editorial brief did not include scouring bargain basements, working out sales tax or fighting off other shoppers. My week-long visit was focussed on one issue: birding.

In the autumn of 1994 I had been given my own birdwatching column on the *Daily Star*, the first of its kind in a British national tabloid newspaper. Some thought it was just another gimmick in the 'red top' circulation war, but for me it was a glorious opportunity to write about a passion that was becoming an ever greater part of my life. Outside work, I was the Secretary of the recently formed Bedfordshire Bird Club and was also writing articles for *Birdwatch* magazine. Although the constraints of a Fleet Street career and a young family meant my UK twitching days had all but disappeared, family holidays and the occasional working trip abroad meant my embryonic global life list was continually being increased by one or two species each year. When the Editor of the *Daily Star* explained that the new column would not be bolstering my pay packet, I was more than happy to write about birds and the birding scene as a labour of love. A growing readers' mailbag – including a few congratulatory letters to the Editor on his decision to provide reading for the birdwatching public – quickly established the column as a weekly mainstay. My efforts were finally rewarded when one of the senior executives agreed to fund the occasional 'Strictly for the Birds' overseas special. There was no doubt about the first destination. I just needed to seek out stories to justify an all-expenses trip to New York.

Slipping past the big yellow taxis, stretch limos, teeming hordes of shoppers, tourists and city workers, in-your-face street signage, street corner salesmen and swaggering cops, I felt strangely at home and at one with the lifestyles being played out in the most frantic city on Earth. I longed to tell my own taxi driver to take me straight to Central Park. It was May, late afternoon, and I could imagine all manner of brilliant birds flitting and flicking their way through newly opened leaf buds. Like the teeming hordes dashing along sidewalks, taking their lives into their hands every time they crossed the canyon-like Manhattan avenues, I had a purpose, a minute-by-minute schedule to stick to if I wanted to squeeze every valuable moment out of the trip.

First item on the agenda was to meet up with the New York 'rat pack' – the cabal of US-based correspondents who kept London in tune with one of the busiest news patches anywhere. I had arranged to meet up with some old British friends and was royally feted that first night at watering holes ingrained in Fleet Street legend. Being a New York 'staff man' is about as good as it gets for a journalist and the hospitality shown to visitors from the old country is always warm and generous. The hit comedy series *Cheers* may have been based in Boston, but the larger-than-life characters I met that night in the Big Apple's finest watering holes could easily have gone head-to-head with Kelsey Grammer, Woody Harrelson, Ted Danson and Kirstie Alley in the comedy stakes. It would have been all too easy to let the socialising interfere with my schedule but I had to be up and away from New York early the next morning. I had to collect a hire car, navigate my way through the labyrinthine road system of upper Manhattan and then head north towards Connecticut for the most eagerly anticipated interview of my life.

A career of button-holing and door-stepping the good and the great of British society had filled countless notebooks with sit-down chats or off-the-cuff quotes from some of the 20th century's most iconic figures. Princess Diana, Margaret Thatcher, Tony Blair and David Cameron are just some of the high-profile figures who have assisted my career with phrases like 'I am delighted' (Princess Diana on the news that the Duchess of York was pregnant) and 'we are delighted' (Mrs Thatcher opening a new food industry research facility with her husband Denis). As I spread out a route map on the passenger seat and placed a cup of hot coffee in the dashboard drinks holder, I thought of the questions and wise words I would be hearing when I kept my interview rendezvous later that afternoon. The interview had taken a great deal of arranging. Publicists had been telephoned, letters sent, copies of my column faxed across the Atlantic. I was meeting American royalty.

Roger Tory Peterson is the greatest birder in history. This genial, upstate New Yorker of Swedish stock is without question birdwatching's most important figure, the innovator, the mastermind, who turned a quaint, humble pursuit into a passion and delight for millions. He was the frontiersman who carved open the unchartered territories of bird identification; he was the brilliant artist who brought to life the colour and vibrancy of garden birds and encouraged folk to venture forth and identify the treasures of marsh and forest; he was the forward thinker who created the birder's new testament, a compact guide that could fit in the pocket and spell out all the clues to a bird's identity with one carefully crafted illustration.

Not that the publishing world was quite ready for Peterson's *A Field Guide to the Birds* when it was first proffered to countless book companies during the dark days of the Great Depression. The Houghton Mifflin company finally gambled and printed 2,000 copies with its dust jacket billing of a 'book on the new plan' – Peterson's revolutionary idea of using pointer arrows to pick out the key field marks on each species such as the white cheek patches on a Canada Goose or the lemon-toned rump of the Myrtle Warbler. Within weeks, it had sold out. New print runs were ordered and more books flew off the shelves to satisfy the demands of a bird-loving nation wanting to put names to their yard birds. Soon an edition concentrating on the Western states was on the market and there followed books on butterflies, bugs, mammals and trees, all using Peterson's 'new plan' pointer system. The concept was also ripe for export. The Collins guide to European birds that I longingly pored over in that Italian book shop in the late Sixties was also decorated with his annotated artwork, his technique now known as the Peterson Identification System. Quite rightly, the American biologist and educator, Paul Ralph Ehrlich, was to say of him: 'In this century, no one has done more to promote an interest in living creatures than Roger Tory Peterson, the inventor of the modern field guide.' Every American award for natural sciences and conservation came his way. There was also the Presidential Medal of Freedom – the highest civilian award in American life – and a host of international honours.

To be granted an hour's audience with this most legendary of figures at his studio home in Old Lyme, a good three hours' drive north from Manhattan, was a great honour. I dare not be late.

The New York rush hour had already put me behind schedule, particularly when I had performed almost two whole circuits of the Harlem district after getting hopelessly lost. Spring squalls had also coalesced into a May monsoon, and my windscreen wipers were working a frantic shift as I finally hit the Connecticut Turnpike, thankful that the rain prevented me from rubber-necking at fly-past bird shapes whose identity I would have loved to have secured. My Peterson was tucked in a briefcase. I arrived at his property with ten minutes to spare and speed read for the hundredth time my briefing notes before heading through gates and a puddle-laced drive, avoiding the heavy drips from the maples, hackberry and hornbeams that cloaked the property. The greeting from his assistant was genial but added to the grandeur of the occasion.

'Dr Peterson will meet you in his study,' she said, leading me away from the main residence and towards a sumptuous wooden building at one with the woods and perfect for engendering inspiration. Inside, it was like an art gallery. Inspiration was manifested in countless illustrations, paintings and half-complete masterpieces propped on easels. There were books and photographs, paints, brushes, curios and knick-knacks that demanded inspection. Only good manners kept me in the comfy seat where I had been told to wait.

At the stroke of 2 p.m., the allotted time for the interview, in walked a tall, slim figure with a shock of white hair carrying a tea tray. I stood in deference, immediately struck by the incredible blue of his eyes. He may have been in his 86th year, his skin weathered by so much time outdoors, but his eyes were a beautiful cerulean colour, the same tones as the warbler I imagined he had heard singing many times from the trees outside.

'English tea,' were my host's first words. 'And cookies, too, although I think you call them biscuits.'

The first ten minutes of the meeting were like a ritualistic Japanese tea ceremony. I held the delicate china cup as if it was a bird's egg and made sure not slurp or spill any of its milky contents. Great painter but could do with a lesson on how to do a good brew, I thought to myself.

Once a clear space had been found for the tea tray, on a small table cluttered with books and papers, we went through the interview formalities. My enthusiastic, perhaps obsequious, gratitude at being granted an interview matched by Dr Peterson's kind words of welcome; he seemed somewhat taken aback that I had travelled all the way from the UK for an hour in his presence. Sixty minutes were nowhere near enough. By the time we had drunk our tea, shared more courtesies, and spoke about Dr Peterson's memories of England and a few wartime experiences, the clock was running down. Even at the age most men have clocked up 20 years' retirement, this incredible figure was still working a 10-hour day. Mornings saw him at his drawing table working on the fifth edition of his eponymous field guide, afternoons were time for his 'interpretive painting', the description he used for the beautifully crafted masterpieces that place him alongside Britain's Archibald Thorburn and Sir Peter Scott and the New World's Louis Agassiz Fuertes and John James Audubon, as the greatest exponents of bird art.

While speaking about his love of framing birds in their natural settings rather than on the blank sheets of a field guide lay out, Dr Peterson walked to the corner of his studio and returned carrying a sumptuous coffee table book and a broad smile. The cover displayed two Northern Flickers squabbling, under the words *Roger Tory Peterson: the Art and Photographs of the World's Foremost Birder*. I wanted to ask if he felt he was the planet's top birder but decided to direct the question to the flickers. I had read they were his favourite bird. Why? Without hesitation, he looked at the time and beckoned me to the door. Had I offended him? Seconds later, we were outside. Sibilant birdsong was trickling through leaves coated in rain drops. Grey skies were easing to blue. Dr Peterson cupped his ear and listened.

'I just heard a flicker,' he said. 'I think you would have enjoyed seeing one.' I raised my eyebrows in agreement, wanting to remain silent as I sensed I was about to be graced with a master class in birdsong identification.

'Weeta weeta weetsee,' a squeaky mouse-like noise greeted us at eye-level. Dr Peterson whispered 'Magnolia Warbler.' Instantly, a glorious grey-and-yellow bird worked its way into the open, displaying its heavily streaked breast as if it was a Regency beau showing off a new frock coat.

Dr Peterson smiled and pointed upwards. 'Rose-breasted Grosbeak. Can you hear its song? It's something like the robin. Not your English one, of course, but the American Robin.' The soft, whispery tones of his voice that had demanded my full concentration during the interview were perfect for in-the-field instruction. 'Weeeep!' A loud whistle brought his instant diagnosis. Great Crested Flycatcher, he called. Sure enough, a bruiser of a flycatcher tumbled through a tangle of dead snags as if it were a heat-seeking missile locked on to some luckless prey item.

Scarlet Tanager, Baltimore Oriole and a cooing Mourning Dove joined the growing afternoon chorus. Dr Peterson continued to introduce the star turns of his home woods like a proud master of ceremonies. Northern Parula and Wilson's and Myrtle Warblers squeaked at frequencies most octogenarians had long lost but the master birder heard and called with a speed that belied his years.

Explaining the song of the parula, a tit-like ball of energy coated in a plumage of blue, green and gold, he said it was like the bird was going up the stairs before tripping over the top. The glorious Chestnut-sided Warbler with its lemony tones accentuated with a rusty 'go fast' stripe, he explained, sang cheerily, 'pleased, pleased, pleased, to meet'cha!'

I mumbled the mnemonic under my breath as the Chestnut-sided continued singing at almost arm's length. Blessed with such a wonderful colour scheme, who could blame it for the flamboyancy of its meet-and-greet rituals? Watching the great birder in action, listening, peering, using his binoculars, was as much an art lesson as if he had been teaching the finer points of shading and perspective. Ethereal sprites high in the canopy seemed to deliver themselves for scrutiny as soon as he called their names. A Solitary Vireo poked its gunmetal blue head out from some dogwood. A Blue-grey Gnatcatcher tiptoed its way through some fluffy blossom, tail twitching instinctively to give balance. I was in the shadow of a giant. How I wished I had his skills, his empathy with nature and the birds he so loved. Another shower sent the canopy foliage rattling like snare drums. My audience with the great man was coming to an end. What made the farewells all the sadder was the realisation that I would never again go birding with him. Yet there was still time for one more moment's example of his generosity of spirit. As I shook hands and thanked him for his time and hospitality, he handed me a signed copy of his beautifully illustrated biography.

'To Stuart, Good Birding! Roger Tory Peterson,' read the inscription written in his distinctive handwriting with ink the colour of the brightest cardinal. For me, it had truly been a red letter day.

The British are Coming
New Jersey, 1995

Looking back and seeing the tall, languid frame of Roger Tory Peterson stroll back to his studio for another evening session with paint brush and palette, I instinctively knew that I would never walk nor talk with the great man again. Sadly, the following year Dr Peterson passed away at his home. He was 87. His legacy today stands proud on the bookshelves of millions and with the work of the Roger Tory Peterson Institute of Natural History that celebrates his name. Of all the glowing eulogies that followed his death, one from another founding father of modern American birding, the writer and conservationist Pete Dunne, I find particularly poignant.

'Roger was fond of saying that God, in all his wisdom, had crafted but two creatures with feathers: birds and angels. God, in his wisdom, gave us Roger Tory Peterson to interpret and instruct us.

And although I do not wish to presume, and I cannot possibly be certain, I have a hunch that by the time I reach the hereafter, there will be a 'Field Guide to the Angels' waiting for me. With luck, it might even be in its second or third edition.'

Pete Dunne's skill with words shows why he is to American ornithological literature what Peterson has been to its bird art. He brings a wonderful spirituality to the science, or should it be art, of nature watching, moulding his craft as a fieldsman of the highest order with an ability to put into words how we feel when nature touches the soul. Besides penning such classics as *Tales of a Low-Rent Birder*, *The Feather Quest* and *Prairie Spring*, Pete has also given us the ultimate in competitive birdwatching – the World Series of Birding. Cynics may say that Americans have a knack of over-hyping their domestic, some may say minority, sports. Its top baseball competition has the 'world series' epithet, while grid-iron football has the Super Bowl and until 1986, the US basketball finals were known as the World Championships. Although the World Series of Birding (WSB) takes place only in the USA (and only in the state of New Jersey, in fact) largely attracts American competitors and is invariably won by Americans, it would be unfair to accuse it of being xenophobic or insular. Over its 27-year history it has raised an incredible $8 million for conservation causes all over the planet and always offers a warm hand of welcome to any overseas competitor who has the key prerequisites of a WSB contender: an intimate knowledge of wood-warbler songs and thrush flight calls; an ability to stay awake for 24-hours-plus, a liking for candy bars and sodas; a knowledge of the back roads of New Jersey and, of course, good bladder control.

When I rang Pete Dunne one cold January night in 1995, asking if I could become a WSB competitor he never mentioned any of the above. Perhaps he thought I would have been scared off. I had taken part in many a county bird race in the UK, but a day-long yomp around the wilds of Bedfordshire's 480 square miles of clay pits, farmland and urban sprawl pales when compared to the WSB's playing field – the 8,722 square miles of New Jersey. In Bedfordshire, clocking up 100 species in 24-hours is a challenge. WSB competitors usually hit the century mark before their breakfast break, and you need a double ton to even get into the top ten teams. That's serious birding, demanding a comprehensive knowledge of North American birds. This is why I guessed I was chancing my luck when I asked Pete if I could compete. Besides taking a Central Park break from my New York shopping expedition three years earlier, I had a virtually no experience of America's Eastern birds.

Far from deterring my approaches, Pete was welcoming, friendly and reassuring. Within days, I learned I was to be the fourth member of a team sponsored by Swift Instruments, a leading American optical company. Muster call was set for midnight on 13 May. The British were coming!

Having been given a wild card to take part in the WSB, I needed to seriously 'gen up' on American birds. Like many birdwatchers, I find preparing for a foreign trip exhilarating, harking back to the days when my father would spread out maps on the dining room table and read out extracts from travel guides on what we should look out for on our family travels. Planning a bird trip itinerary is one thing, preparing to take part in a bird race increases the stakes exponentially. I first had to learn what birds were present in New Jersey's myriad of habitat types; then I had to research their field marks, flight patterns and behaviour before finally getting to grips with their songs and calls... In short, I was cramming 25 years' life-learning into a four month crash course. Every leisure moment that spring saw me scouring bird books or listening to another excellent identification aid from the Peterson Field Guides stable, the *Birding by Ear* cassette tapes. To improve not only my aural skills but also to simply get to grips with scores of new species I had never encountered before, I developed an array of mnemonics to help me remember the songs and also make sense of the regiments of songbirds displayed in field guides like suspects on a police line-up.

One trick I found useful for remembering the various genera of wood-warblers was to take a species' name and liken it to a Wild West figure or a landscape feature. Hence, the *Oporornis* warbler with black face markings that looked like Davy Crockett's sideburns was the Kentucky Warbler. Similarly, the small, yellowish *Dendroica* with a trail of black 'wagonwheel marks' along its flanks must be a Prairie Warbler. Soon I had a series of bizarre devices for helping me to remember dozens of species by likening their field characteristics and names to a whole range of wild and wacky cowboys, western films and place names, most of which I would be embarrassed to repeat. Slowly, the revision sessions taken on the train ride to work, during meal times, in the bath, in front of the television and at bedtime began to be downloaded to the memory banks. I used to get the children to test me by putting their hands over the bird names as I reeled off a page of vireos and thrushes or get my wife to read out a description of a bird which I would attempt to identify before she finished reading. By 1 May, I thought I was ready to become a WSB contestant. Roger Tory Peterson's garden master class 11 days later showed I was still seriously lacking in the basic hear-spot-identify process that birders take for granted on their home patches. I knew I had a lot to learn, perhaps too much, but I had a more immediate problem: my tight agenda in the USA meant I was taking part in the WSB just hours after the interview with Roger Tory Peterson in upstate Connecticut. Before competition commenced, the first challenge was to get across New York in the evening rush hour. Sting and Gershwin had accompanied my first attack on New York but now it was right-wing talk radio shows that kept my eyelids from slowly squeezing together as I slithered to the start line of the 1995 World Series of Birding. The hypnotic glare of red tail lights would have sent me to sleep had it not been for the firebrand ranting coming over the car's stereo sound system. CJ from Palookaville was calling for a holy crusade against the Jihadists and Ellie-Sue, who sounded all of 18, wanted to know where she could get a .5 Desert Eagle handgun as featured in the big action movie, *Under Siege 2*. News updates and traffic alerts also kept me awake although the announcers' speed of delivery and the East Coast accents, along with mention of place names I never knew I never knew, were of little help in navigating one of the planet's busiest road networks as the Friday night traffic converged into a morass of flashing brake lights.

My challenge was to skirt Manhattan, hit the Bronx and then take the double-decker George Washington Bridge into New Jersey, where my teammates were waiting. All was going well until hunger pangs fanned by almost 24 hours without food, apart from Dr Peterson's homemade cookies, began to send my energy reserves plummeting. I pulled off the main Interstate 95 looking for a fast food outlet to silence the tummy rumbling. Bad mistake. The rack of ribs and fries served up in a back street steakhouse in some anonymous commuter town were as tasty as the waitresses were sassy. I cleaned the ribs faster than a Turkey Vulture, washing the meal down with the most delectable glass of beer I've ever tasted, its sweet, honey aroma complementing the rib marinade. As soon as I finished, I called the barmaid over and asked for another glass. She hurried away whispering to herself and returned with a business card, which she placed on the table with a thump.

'Have you a problem with intoxicating liquor?' The card shouted in bold letters. 'Do you need help? If so, call...'

By the time I read the card, the entire restaurant, chefs, waitresses and customers, were looking my way.

'The manager has refused you any more to drink,' the once flirtatious waitress pronounced with the air of a school ma'am. 'He thinks you might need help.'

In the background I could hear fellow diners using the words 'British' and 'drinking' in the same sentence. I had consumed one measly tea cup-size glass of beer, alcohol content less than three per cent, but I found myself branded some kind of barfly. I asked for the bill – checks are what you get in chess, I told the waitress – counted out what was owed in dimes, nickels and quarters, and stormed off without leaving a tip. My fit of pique created more whispers; it also left me hopelessly lost as I drove off without giving any thought of the roads I had taken when I arrived and where I needed to head. Three hours later, having got hopelessly lost on suburban New York's tortuous road network and survived a bumper-shunt with a large Lincoln Continental driven by two giants who could easily have got jobs impersonating the A-Team's Mr T, I was almost at the WSB start line.

Start line was perhaps something of a misnomer. The WSB doesn't begin with the crack of a pistol and a Le Mans style sprint to revving vehicles. The 50 or so four-man teams can begin their bird tallying anywhere within the state boundary as long as their completed checklists are delivered to the Cape May race headquarters – 145 or so miles as the American Crow flies due south from the spot where I was standing – before the stroke of midnight. I had arrived at the home of the Swift Fliers captain Rob Unrath, exhausted and emotionally drained. Having to drive for hours on end and then talk my way out of a minor traffic prang looking up at two unamused, muscle-bound guys a whole foot taller than me was hardly the right preparation for the arduous challenge ahead. Rob, a genial supermarket manager, put me at ease, welcoming me like a long-lost relative with a firm handshake and a cheery smile, dismissing my apologies for being late with an understanding nod.

Making up for lost time, I was soon to learn, was a particular forte of this highly organised and expert birder. Already he had a minute-by-minute schedule worked out. Rather than scour the entire state, we would be concentrating on just two of New Jersey's 21 counties. Although the decision meant we could not win the big prize – the state-wide competition – I was more optimistic that with Rob's intimate knowledge of the marshes, swamps, parks, farmland, forests and, importantly, urban sprawl, we would be still be seeing lots of birds, and I would be getting plenty of life ticks. Having said hello and goodbye to Rob's delightful family in almost the same breath, we headed from his home in a sedate suburban neighbourhood towards the New Jersey Meadowlands to meet our driver, former policeman Jim Bangma, and Ann 'AJ' Johnson, who put my driving ordeal to shame by motoring an incredible 17 hours from Iowa to be there as the clock edged towards the midnight hour and we could start counting the birds.

I was primed. Bins around my neck, scope at the ready. Our 4x4 was loaded with enough Gatorade and Snickers to fuel a military operation. The squalls that had punctuated my afternoon walk with Dr Peterson a hundred miles to the north had long faded and the faintest of warm breezes ruffled the few strands of vegetation I could make out in the darkness. I had no idea where I was standing, where we were going or what I was supposed to do. Squeaks, squawks and cries were echoing under a starry firmament but it was anyone's guess what creatures were making the noises – birds, mammals, amphibians, or mobsters! The direction we had driven from Rob's home towards the distant glow of Manhattan's late night light pollution, as well as the almost non-stop clamour of distant police car sirens, meant we were not far from human habitation. My eyes could make out man-made shapes, perhaps warehouses or factories. There was the gurgle of running water. I assumed we were somewhere birdy.

Ten, nine, eight... Rob counted down the final seconds to midnight. As soon as the second hand had entered a new day, 13 May 1995, to be exact, the running commentary began. Rob had better ears than any CIA listening base.

'American Coot, Virginia Rail, Sora...' He rattled off names of birds he was hearing with the speed of a tobacco auctioneer. The race had begun and I was already lagging and flagging. The Americans moved like well-coached basketball players imposing a full court press defence strategy. Each one knew what to do without fuss. Rob called the locations, Jim arrived within seconds of the ETA printed on his running sheet and then the three of them decamped, looked, listened and began reeling off the birds, subject to the regulations of the competition. Cricket seems a simple parlour game compared to the rule-heavy WSB. Space prevents detailing anything but the guiding principles: see or hear a species; cause it no harm or disturbance; and then tick it!

As it is a team competition, there is one other key clause the so-called 95 per cent rule. This stipulates that all members of the team, the minimum number being three, must see or hear 19 out of every 20 species encountered for them to count on the final tally. That's serious synchronicity. Look the wrong way when the rest of the team is focussing on some furtive blighter deep in cover, and you've lost a tick on the score card. This explains why most of the crosses on the score cards are 'heard birds'. It is so much easier for a group to latch on to a bird call or burst of song than to get three out of four pairs of binoculars focussed on a distant speck that may or may not be a raptor. Immediately, I found the going tough. Listening to pristine recordings through earphones may have provided the theoretical background at home in the UK; the practical exam amid the forests and marshes of New Jersey was a far greater challenge. Five months after Pete Dunne had found me a place on the birding frontline I was slowly realising I had volunteered for a mission near- impossible.

Place names such as the Hackensack Meadowlands, Kearny Marsh and the Allendale Celery Farm are forever enshrined in my memory without me remembering exactly what I heard or saw there. We would arrive, jump from the vehicle, listen for a few moments and soon Rob would have a bevy of new ticks. From the start, the team realised that I was more of a handicap than an asset, but, in keeping with the rules, they made every effort to not only ensure that I had heard a certain burst of bird noise, but also to explain which bird had made it. I was soon catching on. The sound of two stones being clicked together resonating deep in some pitch black bog was the song of the tiny Yellow Crake. An eerie 'who-cooks-for-me-who-cooks-for-you' that boomed from a wooded hillside still drenched in darkness was the song of the Barred Owl.

As the first rays of a new day broke on the eastern horizon, they acted like a conductor's baton bringing the string section together, the crake check-out and owl prowl were abandoned, the songbirds were getting in tune for the dawn chorus. In the gloom Rob beamed.

'This is where it gets fun,' he smiled as we climbed back into the vehicle and headed away from the lowlands for the deciduous woods and pine forests that give New Jersey such a cosmopolitan bird list. Take a walk through a highly managed English wood in spring and you may be lucky to hear a handful of warblers, a few thrushes, tits and a sprinkling of other species, such as Eurasian Nuthatch and Common Treecreeper, over an hour or so. In contrast, American species are attracted to the subtle niches that occur in woodland, with individuals, particularly the wood-warblers, having a wish list of micro-habitat prerequisites. Rob and Jim's knowledge of their birds and the back roads of Passaic and Bergen counties meant we could target species by each bird's favourite suite of requirements. For instance, the gorgeous Golden-winged Warbler – arguably the most beautiful of all the American passerines to have arrived on

British soil – loves stunted, new-growth tracts of forest, an environment readily produced when power lines are cut through prime woodland.

We arrived at a suitable site, a once attractive hillside gouged to make way for a row of incongruous pylons. Within seconds, a buzzy 'zee bee bee bee' was lisping deep within cover. Rob, Jim and AJ indicated they had all connected with the bird with raised thumbs. So had I, but I wanted to linger, to see and savour this gold-plated beauty that had become such a thing of legend back home, especially as I had missed the solitary British occurrence, the so-called 'Tesco bird', which created the biggest twitch in history when one turned up in a supermarket car park at Maidstone, Kent, in 1989. The warbler scurried and created flickers of leaf movement. I got miniscule glimpses of its form in the murky dawn light. Goldie sang again and again, its high-pitched buzzes tempting me to throw the clockwork precision of the team's itinerary so that I could indulge in the glory of its colour scheme. I was called to order. There were scores more birds to 'see' (read hear).

With ruthless efficiency we worked our way through the warbler pages, up and down the vireo plates and then began ticking off most of the illustrations under the thrushes section of my Peterson guide (signed by the great man himself). We ticked off woodpeckers and collected a cartload of sparrows. The harsh tones of the Red-winged Blackbird seemed to greet us every time we got out of the vehicle. Baltimore Orioles and Rose-breasted Grosbeaks brought colours and shapes to a running total that was still dominated by sound-only encounters. A Scarlet Tanager gleamed from a head height branch like a shop's neon sign. Tiny, frustrating 'Empids' – a complex of five flycatchers in the genus *Empidonax* found in the Eastern states that strains the skills of the greatest American birders – proved, well, complex. American Kestrels, Broad-winged and Red-tailed Hawks and two accipiters, Sharp-shinned and Cooper's

Hawks, ensured the checklist's birds of prey section was beginning to fill with crosses. Overhead, squadrons of the ubiquitous Turkey Vulture cast menacing shadows, a reminder that they were ready to pounce and pick to the bone any WSB straggler.

The 100th bird of the day – I cannot remember the species, my attempts to keep a personal tally had long been abandoned – came and went long before noon. Great Northern Divers, a far more romantic name than the Common Loon the Americans used, glided through still waters coated with a diaphanous haze, their eerie love song raising the hairs on my neck. A noisy Upland Sandpiper, a rare and elusive pastureland bird all but extinct in the state, also stretched its vocal chords with bubbly song. The journey took us to stakeouts that Rob and Jim knew from their detailed reconnoitres in previous days and also to locations with a reputation for always producing good birds. At one reliable lookout spot I was consumed watching a flock of Cedar Waxwings when the others latched on to a distant Bald Eagle. I responded instantly to their frantic calls as the giant black form slowly disappeared out of view, but failed to see it in time. For the others, it was yet another species to be considered under the 95 per cent rule, due to my failings. I was gutted for them and also for myself. Bald Eagle, the national bird, a potent symbol of American power and also one of my most eagerly sought sightings, had escaped my attentions by a millisecond. Gloom filled me as we peeled off the wrappers of our Snickers bars and refuelled with Gatorade. The sun's position in the afternoon sky was a signal to head back to the Meadowlands.

Driving away from the wild, back roads where Black Bears and Eastern Coyote patrol and the sharp quills of roadkill Porcupine are a constant puncture threat, it was difficult to believe that New Jersey is the most densely populated state in the Union with almost nine million residents. Within half an hour, the impenetrable forests were thinning out and spacious clapboard homesteads set in stands of hornbeam and maple were appearing with increasing regularity. Suburbia came and went and soon we were driving through true urban sprawl, mostly affluent neighbourhoods with shiny, new cars and fluttering Stars and Stripes, though occasionally we hit blocks with ugly, graffiti-scrawled buildings and sad, aimless characters who had long accepted that the American dream was just that. Unprepossessing factory units, soulless shopping parades and billboards championing television series yet to grace British screens continued to flash by and traffic lights became more frequent. Green road signs pointed to place names from songs and movies – Union City, Jersey City and Hoboken, the birthplace of Frank Sinatra – and began channelling us towards America's most iconic symbol.

Frédéric Bartholdi's colossus stands proudly in the mouth of the New York Harbour, a welcoming sight to the huddled masses of the European diaspora since 1886. The Statue of Liberty is truly an awesome modern wonder, 300 feet from plinth to flaming torch and framed by the distant towering skyscrapers of downtown Manhattan. However, I could pay only cursory homage by way of a couple of happy snaps to show my children back home, we were running against the clock and there was a different type of sightseeing to be done. Beneath Libertas, as the giant sculpture is known, birds were bobbing in estuarine waters made choppy by countless tourist vessels. With my scope cranked up to maximum zoom and the experience of many misspent years looking out over reservoirs and brick pits under my belt, I felt I could finally begin making a contribution to the team effort. A black-capped Bonaparte's Gull flashed its distinctive wing pattern as it avoided being mugged by greedy Ring-billed Gulls. Great Black-backed and American Herring Gulls loitered for bigger pickings. Greater and Lesser Scaup kept themselves apart out on the water but still made for convenient comparisons and positive identifications. As an ornate grebe broke the surface, the afternoon light caught its golden 'horns' and I immediately shouted 'Slav!' There was no response from my teammates until it dawned: I was speaking a different birding language. I tried again, this time saying 'Horned Grebe at 75 yards' and elicited a far different response. Back slaps and cries of that greatest of American birding compliments – 'good call' – filled me with that warming feeling of pride that only a birdwatcher truly appreciates. When I picked out a solitary Arctic Tern among a mixed flock of Common and Forster's Terns, a scarce bird on Eastern Seaboard in spring, I was no longer a Limey interloper. Stu the Brit Birder had finally arrived.

We left behind the hordes of tourists at the Liberty State Park, many bemused at the sight of four sightseers getting more excited about the 'seagulls' than the incredible bronze statue that dominated the waterscape. Heading north above the steep bluffs that overlook the Hudson River, Jim laughed as he explained that we would not have to worry about the crowds at the next venue, a small wooded park in a sedate residential area that had gained local notoriety as a migrant hotspot. Time was against us. Clutching our binoculars and another round of candy bars, we dashed past rows of sumptuous town houses with ornate gated drives and landscaped gardens. Mid-sprint, I remembered my scope was in full view on the back seat of the 4x4. I instinctively turned to cover it up, only for Jim to tell me I need not worry.

This was supposedly where New Jersey's 'made men' – the so-called Mafia wise guys who would become immortalised in *The Sopranos* in the following decade – resided with their surgically enhanced molls and ill-gotten gains. Understandably, car thefts and petty crime were unknown. Even dropping a candy wrapper on the pristine sidewalks was likely to see you sleeping with the fishes in the nearby Hudson. Birds and birders seemed to be tolerated, which was fortunate as we could easily have overstayed our welcome while enjoying the beautiful monochrome tones of a Blackpoll Warbler that had taken time out from its long flight to the Canadian forest belt to deliver bursts of its screechy, high-pitched song. The local Peregrine that spent its time commuting across the Hudson River to harass Manhattan's pigeon population, however, failed to show and so we headed back to the place where we had begun our chase some 16 hours earlier – the Meadowlands.

At midnight, the place was a dark mire of unfathomable noises and foreboding. For all its uninviting qualities, with the presence of a railway track and busy turnpike, in daylight Kearny Marsh was a shorebird lover's heaven. Lesser and Greater Yellowlegs waded in the shallow freshwater lagoons and Semipalmated Sandpipers pitter-patted alongside diminutive Least Sandpipers and long-billed *hudsonia* race Dunlins in the muddy margins. A smart blue-billed Ruddy Duck bubbled to its mate and a small flock of Blue-winged Teal displayed intricate face-markings that could have been applied by a make-up artist. A solitary Great Blue Heron kept a watchful eye on proceedings as daylight began to fade. The growing shorebird tally filled out the largest expanse of blank spaces on our running list. There was time for just one more stop at Hackensack before the loss of sunlight made viewing impossible. Evening morphed into night and the wispy fronds of a vast expanse of phragmites slowly disappeared from sight. The haunting sounds of the reed bed began to echo once more.

Amphibians and birds impersonating amphibians croaked and peeped, invisible creatures scurried through the marshy vegetation, splashing and squealing. We were on a mission for two valuable ticks for our race tally, birds that would both be lifers for me and, indeed, rank among the most eagerly sought by any British birder. Our 22-hour birding endurance challenge had come to an end but there was still one final hurdle, a 120-mile drive to the southernmost point of New Jersey – Cape May, arguably the most famous birding locale anywhere in the world. To have our complete checklist verified, the whole team had to be present at the WSB nerve centre before midnight. I was glad not to be driving. After more than 40 hours awake, apart from a few quickly snatched moments of shut-eye in the back of the vehicle, I was so consumed by tiredness and fatigue that I relaxed in the back seat and began to compose my first ever birding dispatch from a foreign location, with bird sounds still resonating in my head. There was the rich, spiralling aria of the Wood Thrush and the joyful carols of American Robins. Mockingbird trills and Brown Thrasher high notes were imprinted on my mind as if they had been recorded tape-to-tape. Together, they formed a beautiful lullaby that lured me into a deep sleep that lasted until we pulled into the car park at the base of Cape May's famous lighthouse.

How did the Swift Fliers' challenge go? The following article, which appeared in the *Daily Star's* 'Strictly for the Birds' column on 19 May 1995, revealed our finishing position.

A ghostly scream shakes the dark, impenetrable forest. It has just turned 2.33 a.m. as the Barred Owl lets rip. Another tick, and we are on our way into the New Jersey night. This is the World Series of Birding and it is the most frantic, draining and enjoyable birdwatching experience of my life.

Only when I'm standing, shivering in a damp forest bog, my trainers covered in slime, do I question my sanity.

Why am I doing this? I ask myself. Then a Golden-winged Warbler bursts into song. I clench my fist and cheer. This will be a race to remember. For the past 11 years, birders from across the USA have migrated on the second Saturday of May for the WSB. It's a megabucks event, with big businesses sponsoring teams. It had always been my dream to take part and I finally got the call. The organisers, New Jersey Audubon Society, had found me a vacancy with a team of top-drawer US birders, sponsored by Swift Instruments. Swift is one of the world's leading binocular and telescope producers.

I meet my teammates a few minutes before midnight and am greeted with a curt: 'We're late!' My three colleagues are supermarket manager Rob Unrath, former policeman Jim Bangma and Ann 'AJ' Johnson, who has driven from her home in Iowa to take part. They're all experts and it shows as they rattle off warblers, hawks, sparrows, rails and orioles, seen or heard, as we criss-cross the countryside.

This year Rob and Jim have decided to limit our birding to a designated area. New Jersey is bigger than Wales, so the right tactics are vital. Time flies. Owls at dawn, woodpeckers at breakfast, thrushes for lunch (metaphorically, of course), then a long haul to the Statue of Liberty for teatime. By this time, 'The Brit' has become 'Stu the Brit Birder'. I really feel part of the team. As the sun sets, we see an American Bittern fly into a marsh and a Common Nighthawk comes out to hunt insects. We tally our birds – 159! But there's still a 140-mile drive to the finish where we must hand in our scorecard by midnight.

The next morning hundreds of birders converge on Cape May's Grand Hotel for the awards ceremony. Then the announcement comes for the teams who have taken a limited route: Swift Instruments – third. Backslapping and handshakes all round. We pulled off a great result. And the competition has raised £300,000 for conservation projects. What an amazing experience. I loved every minute – and I just cannot wait for next May to do it all over again.

There were no cups or medals for our third place but going by the reaction of the hundreds of fellow competitors at the awards brunch our efforts were widely applauded. The fact that the Swift team had a novice birder in their midst made the achievement all the more surprising, particularly as I had boosted my life list by an astonishing 35 new species. There was one downside. I found myself in Cape May, the capital of American birding, arguably the most birdwatcher-friendly place in the world, where even the high street shops are adorned with birding paraphernalia, and we had to leave. Almost as soon as the awards ceremony finished, I was ushered back to our vehicle for the long drive back north. I had a flight back to the UK to catch.

As we drove past a row of gaily painted antebellum houses that looked as if they had been used for the backdrop of *Pollyanna*, I looked longingly at the bird feeders and Purple Martin nest-boxes and remembered the words of the famous American general, Douglas Macarthur. I would return.

Rich Man, Poor Man

Gambia, 2000

The dark despair of loneliness came down quicker than an African sunset. Two days' sublime birding had come to an end and as I waved goodbye to my new friends, I felt as if every good feeling in my life had been sucked away. I had never been predisposed to depression but having read Sylvia Plath's *The Bell Jar* as a mixed-up, lonely student, I began to sense that I was trapped in a hermetically sealed container of despondency and the tight constrictions of my moods were squeezing out all hope and optimism.

Forty-eight hours earlier, I could not have been more excited. Beautiful Abyssinian Rollers, almost identical twins to the European model but with incongruous, ornate tails, provided the welcoming committee as I stepped off the late afternoon charter flight from London and on to the African continent for the first time in my life. Birding friends had joked I was experiencing 'Africa

Lite' when I told them I had agreed to write a travel feature about Gambia's burgeoning tourist industry. Jibes that the former British colony and smallest country in Africa was too westernised, too commercialised, to sense the heartbeat and the soul of real sub-Saharan Africa had left me thinking I was about to visit some kind of Spanish Costa. My first footfall on the warm, concrete apron at Banjul Airport, decorated with swirling shadows cast by the countless Hooded Vultures overhead, left me in no doubt that I was not only entering a wholly new birding dimension, but that I had arrived somewhere very different, and very special.

The sweaty arrivals lounge was a heaving mass of oversize suitcases, giant cardboard parcels containing televisions and sound systems, taxi drivers holding signs with badly spelt English-sounding names, and smart businessmen and women dressed in brightly coloured grandmuba costumes made from metres of cloth wrapped around the body as the dress code demands in this most modest of countries. The room was also full of young men pleading for copies of English newspapers. Football, especially the Premiership, is as popular in West Africa as it is in working men's clubs and pubs back home in Britain and, for young African fans, there is no better place to find out the latest scores and transfer movement news as the hot-off-the press tabloids brought in weekly by waves of European tourists. As soon as one young man dressed in an Arsenal football shirt saw that I was carrying a bundle of the day's newspapers under one arm while trying to juggle my luggage in the other, he homed in with a broad, toothy grin...

'Toubab, Toubab, can I have your papers? I'll pay good money,' he pleaded, his eyes trying to pick out a back page headline on one of the half-dozen copies pressed under my arm.

'I don't talk to Arsenal fans,' I fired back as a joke.

'Why? Who do you support? Man U?' He looked offended.

'Nah, Tott'nam,' I responded in my best North Londonese.

'Tottenham Hotspur?' His diction was perfect. He whistled through his equally perfect white teeth

'But they are not a very good team, Toubab. You should support Arsenal...' He then suddenly burst into the Italian classic, 'Volare', but with his own lyrics.

Vieira, oh, oh... Vieira, oh, oh, oh, oh...

He comes from Senegal, plays for the Arsenal...

I could not help but laugh. Patrick Vieira, scourge of my team Tottenham Hotspur, arguably the best defensive midfielder in the world as well as a son of neighbouring Senegal, appeared to be a god in these parts. As the Gambian Gooner, as he called himself, sang full voice, he turned around to show off of the reverse side of his Arsenal shirt. 'Vieira' and a large number 4 were emblazoned across the back.

Such is the rivalry between north London's two football clubs that even talking to 'The Enemy', one of my fanatical Spurs-supporting father's more polite terms for Arsenal, could be regarded as an act of supreme treachery. But my newfound friend, who was now fighting off the attentions of other youngsters keen to get their hands on my newspapers, had such an endearing way about him that I could not refuse his now desperate pleas.

Clambering on to a coach, I placed the bundle into his leathery hands, but before fully letting go, I had one question:

'What does Toubab mean? Why did you call me it?' I was intrigued.

'That's what we call all Englishmen,' he replied with an air of innocence and honesty. 'But it's not really Toubab, it's Two Bob!'

'Two Bob?' I replied, imitating his well-pronounced vowels.

'Yes...'

He was just about to explain the phrase's origins when the coach door hydraulics gave a wheeze. The driver looked angry and urged me aboard.

'See you, Toubab,' he said with a wave of the rolled up bundle of tabloids. 'Thanks for the papers! *Vieira, Oh, Oh, Oh, Oh...*'

I never knew his name but he was one of the most decent Arsenal fans I've ever met.

Sleep was a poor bedfellow that night. I had seen so many rollers, falcons and other intriguing silhouettes perched up on spindly acacias during the late-evening coach ride to my hotel to know that I was about to enter a new path on my birding rites of passage. I had felt the same bubbling, pre-match tension on that summer's morning in California almost a decade before, the wonderful sense of expectation and awe, knowing that I would soon be watching birds in the flesh that at that moment still remained two-dimensional illustrations in Clive Barlow and Tim Wacher's *Field Guide to the Birds of the Gambia and Senegal.*

The book, with its neat illustrations by Tony Disley, had been constant reading since I had made plans to meet up with a good friend and popular bird guide Peter Dedicoat, who was leading a group on a two-week Gambia–Senegal adventure for a leading British tour company. My own itinerary meant I would only be with them for the first 48 hours when they were based on the coast, at the epicentre of the Gambian tourist industry. Peter promised great birds and was as good as his word. Within an hour of meeting up we were trudging through the dense coastal forest of the Abuko Nature Reserve, thought by many to be the most important and productive birding site in the country.

The reserve's protective fence may only surround 105 hectares of gallery forest and Guinea savannah, but the wildlife is as rich and varied as anywhere in West Africa. Day-trippers from the coastal resorts seeking African big game may feel a little disappointed but for those serious about birds there cannot be a better introduction to the vivid colours and weird and wonderful sounds of the continent's teeming bird life. As soon as we entered the reserve, the ringing chimes of Common Wattle-eyes rippled through the leaves; the male's smooth crooning followed by the buzzy response of his mate. Despite the striking black-and-white tones, a colour scheme that contrasts perfectly with the vermilion red 'eye make-up' – an area of bright, red flesh that stretches across the brow – these small, furtive insect-eaters are perfectly camouflaged for a life foraging amid the dappled light of the forest under-storey.

Wattle-eye song set the background beat to the forest's full chorus, but for newly arrived birders it is sightings rather than aural experiences that really count. Although tropical forests are arguably the toughest of all habitats to work, Abuko was willing to give up its riches in keeping with its reputation as one of the best tourist attractions in Gambia, but this was not some kind of birding zoo.

The Nile Crocodiles that looked so indolent as they lazed about in the pond in front of the reserve's photographic hide would have made short shrift of any sightseer too wrapped up in experiencing the incredible forest sites to be alert to the dangers that lurked only inches away. Another peril came in the coiling shape of the tree-loving Green Mamba, a highly venomous snake supposedly present in good numbers on the reserve along with the equally deadly and infamous Royal Puff Adder and Black-necked Cobra that lurked on the forest floor. Following basic fieldcraft – looking where you step, keeping to marked trails and remembering not to touch anything – meant there were no unfortunate incidents as we traipsed solemnly through the dense rainforest as if we were the first Europeans ever to step foot on its carpet of leaf-litter. Indeed, apart from a few sleepy crocs, lots of scurrying Gambian Sun Squirrels and the occasional glimpses of Red Colubus Monkeys, looking for birds consumed three hours all too quickly, certainly too fast to keep up note-taking or conferring regularly with the field guide that I kept tucked in the waist band of my shorts for supposedly easy reference.

With Pete and one of Gambia's top guides, Sering Bojang, on hand to pick out and identify species before most of us could focus our binoculars, the morning's tally began to look impressive. Every few yards the party was brought to a halt by something new. Brightly coloured Malachite and Blue-breasted Kingfishers; preposterous African Pied Hornbills; African Golden Orioles, as glistening as but subtly different from the European species; a skulking Snowy-crowned Robin-Chat along with a brilliant green-and-yellow Collared Sunbird and a subtly marked but endearing Lesser Honeyguide were just a few of the species that had me trying to juggle my binoculars and field guide.

A Red-bellied Paradise Flycatcher, perched on a snag and displaying its flamboyant terracotta-toned tail, remained the bird of the morning until two Violet Turacos, the colour of Cadbury's chocolate wrappers and with striking scarlet wing flashes, were picked out moving through the canopy. For a novice tropical birder – my only previous rainforest birding had been on Trinidad – the experience was causing an information overload, but when a Blue-cheeked Bee-eater, a new bird and one that had high twitching currency back home in Britain, dashed across a forest clearing, I knew my decision to visit Gambia – Africa lite or not – had been worthwhile.

For a change of afternoon scenery, we turned our attentions to the impenetrable mangrove swamps that skirt the Gambia River where we found the scarce Red-winged Warbler, a top target bird for those African veterans on the tour. Once again, my personal highlight was seeing two Willow Warblers, birds that may well have bred on my local patch back home in Britain and seemed so out of place picking at insects in the heat and humidity of a tropical swamp rather than a Bedfordshire chalk downland. If I was to question myself about whether I was really engaging with the African experience, the answer came the next morning when we picked up Sering at his village home. His eyes and ears had already impressed immensely, but all he needed to do for another highly desired tour sighting was point to the tree outside his house to reveal the daytime roost of a delightful but slightly startled White-faced Scops Owl.

An hour or so later, Sering's knowledge of the local owls and their calls paid amazing dividends when he showed off his incredible mimicry skills. Seconds after giving a few shrill notes of the Pearl-spotted Owlet, he turned a patch of woody scrubland into a heaving maelstrom of small birds, all anxious to mob what they perceived was a predatory intruder. The varied mix of woodland habitats, garnished with rice fields and open savannah, allowed us to add Vieillot's and Bearded Barbets, Striped Kingfisher, Didric Cuckoo and Fine-spotted Woodpecker to the trip list along with Northern Puffback, an impressive shrike-like bird with a black face, fiery red eye and a fluffy white powder-puff of a rump.

The area was not just good for birders. Two foreign hunters, accompanied by a local Gambian, had been at work looking for one of our targets, the highly elusive Double-spurred Francolin. I never saw the shooting party at work but Peter later admitted to me they had been more successful in tracking down this highly sought-after species than we had and had bagged at least one of these partridge-like birds with their bold, teardrop-marked chest and two barbed spurs on each heel.

On the way back to our hotel base, we dropped Sering back off in his home village of Lamin, but not before he had directed the coach driver to a recently harvested peanut field where two Temminck's Coursers, beautifully marked birds with a rusty crown and chest pattern set off by their overall biscuit-coloured tones, competed with the Black-headed Lapwings for our attentions. The sight of two ghostly Black-shouldered Kites quartering a distant field bathed in the soft apricot tones of sunset made for a perfect end to the day. Only then did it strike me: the next day Peter, Sering and their party were departing up river. I would be on my own.

The next morning I sat alone, not inside a bell jar but a bland, soulless hotel room with only Douglas Coupland's thought-provoking but harrowing novel, *Miss Wyoming*, for company. I wished I were home in Britain. The good company and good birds seen over the previous two days seemed an age away. Now I was stuck with no transport and the knowledge that if I stepped outside the hotel complex I would be harangued and followed by all and sundry wanting to show me birds – for a price. Gambia's allure for Westerners as the perfect introduction to African birds had created a cottage industry of wannabe guides, many of whom did not know the end of a beak from the tip of a rectrice. I had already run the gauntlet of guides-for-hire when passing through the heart of the bustling Kotu beach resort the two previous evenings, at the same time side-stepping women fruit-sellers and all manner of hawkers selling typical tourist tat. The wide-eyed pleas of children dressed in charity shop hand-me-downs tugged at the heartstrings. Seeing their smiling faces and hearing their infectious 'thank you, Toubab' was always worth a fistful of coins, but I had no intention of handing over money to guides that did not know even the commonest birds. My patience and humanity seemed to have vanished along with all feelings of sanguinity that I had felt coming down the aircraft steps. I knew I was being mean and hard-hearted, that a few of my tourist pounds would have gone so far in the hands of a local Gambian, but I could not face another call of 'Toubab'. My only recourse was to try and book a scheduled flight back home. Even that would require leaving the hotel room.

I stayed in bed most of the morning, missing breakfast, reading my book and becoming ever more morose. When the maids came, I sat outside watching the Grey-headed Sparrows squabble over the few desiccated crusts left over from the previous day. What struck me about the sparrows was that there appeared to be no females present. Each bird was a combination of slate grey head and chest contrasting with rusty wings, tail and rump. I thought I detected a white throat and instinctively returned to my room to get my binoculars and field guide. Moments later, I was focussing on the sparrows' finer plumage details such as the subtle rusty fringes to the tertials and looking for fine white tips to the median coverts featured in the book. I was turning a ubiquitous yard bird into a thing of beauty. I also learned from the guide that like Tree Sparrows, and unlike House Sparrows, there was no apparent sexual dimorphism; male and female Grey-headed Sparrows look identical. The sparrows disappeared with the remaining crumbs but more birds began gracing the hotel grounds. A pair of Laughing Doves shuffled along a paved area like a couple of old folk on dodgy legs trying to make their way to the shops. Overhead, a medium-size gull was showing enough tantalising glimpses of its underwing pattern for me to rule out Black-headed and decide on Grey-headed. A chic size-zero swift stormed through, its body hardly thicker than the two long tail streamers that trailed in its wake. It could only have been an African Palm Swift. Slowly but surely, my birding mojo was escaping the bite of the black dog mood that had left me wanting to fly back to the UK. I went back to my room, picked up my scope and began walking.

With a new confidence, I passed the hawkers and fruit sellers, paid little heed to the guides lined up on Kotu Bridge, ignored children calling out for pens and sweets and headed away from the resort and into the country. A taxi driver pulled up and asked if I wanted a lift. I pretended I had not heard him and continued walking purposefully along the main road out of Kotu until I came to a path that snaked into lush, open fields liberally sprinkled with palm trees. Cattle Egrets were working the soil like farm labourers under the watchful gaze of Pied Crows that reminded me of parish vicars in their weekday ministerial fatigues. An African Harrier-Hawk upset the calm when it dive-bombed the leafy crown of a palm tree and emerged clutching a small Green Woodhoopoe chick in its lemon-coloured talons. On a small murky pool, an African Black Crake moved in such a mechanical way it could well have been wound up by a clockwork key and set loose to patter around in the mud. Almost as soon as its bright red legs and yellow bill disappeared into the densest sedges, a Greater Painted-Snipe took to the air for a few fleeting moments before dropping back down into the impenetrable vegetation. The momentary glimpse was enough time to make out the heavily patterned wings and strongly marked face of a male bird, its need for cryptic plumage explained by the fact that it undertakes the incubation while its flirty, polyandrous mate finds other males to seduce.

Birding was proving a wonderful tonic to a mood that still hung heavy. As I surveyed the woods and wetland for new areas to explore, there was crash of vegetation behind me and out from nowhere marched a middle-aged man in a bygone season's Manchester United shirt. I froze. He was holding a machete that could easily have sliced the head off of an ox, and the weapon looked all the more menacing when the sun caught its recently sharpened cutting edge. The man spoke Mandinka but I did not need a translator. His ebony eyes reflected his inner anger. He wanted to know why I was trespassing. I was about to speak but remembered that by simply playing ignorant the villagers had left me alone. Much to my chagrin, I fine-tuned the tactic and began mumbling like a deaf mute. The farmer looked nonplussed, perhaps even embarrassed, as I mouthed, 'I am watching birds,' and pointed to my binoculars.

'I'll show you birds.' The man spoke in hesitant English, punctuating the sentence by rubbing his index finger and thumb, the international sign that he wanted paying.

I mumbled an incoherent reply.

There was a long, tense pause before the farmer put down his machete and leaned forward to gently grip my hand. He spoke, his words friendly and soothing and then he led me off the path back the way he had come. We walked hand-in-hand for ten minutes through the bush until we came to a stand of tall hardwood trees. My captor halted, took a step or two back and gripped my shoulders as if to position me. He then stood behind me and slowly lifted my chin so that I was looking up at 45 degrees. There above us sat a kingfisher, the biggest kingfisher I had ever seen, a bird with a dagger-like bill that seemed as sharp and fearsome as the machete I had been confronted with a few moments earlier. I raised my binoculars and studied the three-toned plumage; the gunmetal-and-white dappled upperparts accentuating the brilliant rusty chest and spotty white belly that singled the bird out as a male Giant Kingfisher. For all its striking coloration, it was perfectly camouflaged in its wooded hideaway, perching statue-like with only the occasional blink of its eye to indicate it was alive. Such encounters with an iconic bird – this is Africa's largest kingfisher and vies with Australia's Laughing Kookaburra for the world title – are invariably greeted with whoops of delight. I was about to show exuberant gratitude to my impromptu guide when I remembered my ruse.

Still pretending to be a deaf mute, I fumbled in my pockets for some crumpled Dalasi bank notes and went to hand them over, but instead of taking them the man pulled his hands away and with an exaggerated nod of his head began to speak – in English.

'No. You poor man...' He spoke slowly and clearly so that I could lip-read his words before finishing the sentence with a warm, friendly smile.

Poor man? Me? I had a £1,000 pair of Swarovski binoculars hanging around my neck. He was wearing a circa 1990 Manchester United shirt. I offered the money again, but again he waved his hands to indicate he did not want my money. Instead, he turned and walked back down the path, leaving me to reflect on my subterfuge. I looked at the amount of money I had offered and it was more than £5, most probably more than two or three days' wages for the farmer, and yet he had refused it because he felt sorry for me because of my perceived handicap. I followed after him, mumbled my thanks and walked away, chastened.

Such a salutary, humbling experience was just the fillip needed to pull me out from under the dark clouds. Over the next few days, I met up with another group of British birders, hired a vehicle and driver, and then birded dawn to dusk. A healthy checklist that included Tawny and Wahlberg's Eagles, Long-tailed Nightjar, four species of roller and Kelp Gull, to name but a few, was testimony to Gambia's excellence as a venue for novices or African old hands.

I was later told that the feelings of depression and paranoia had most likely been caused by the strong anti-malarial drugs I had been taking. Luckily, the Grey-headed Sparrows and that unknown Manchester United fan deep in the bush had turned my holiday around. I had almost returned to the UK but instead had been left with countless wonderful memories. Undoubtedly, the most memorable experience was driving through villages and hearing the children laugh and scream out 'Minty' as we threw handfuls of sweets in their direction from our open-top 4x4, a routine that regularly left me covered in red dust and blackened smoke particles.

Back home in Britain, the smoky aroma of village wood fires and the dust from Gambia's blood red soil not only lingered on my clothes but also in my heart.

Only when I returned home did I discover possible meanings for 'Toubab'. Some claim it is a corruption of the Wolof word for Europe. A seasoned African birder explained that it was the word for white people, thought to be derived from 'two bob', which was the going rate for an errand when Gambia was a British colony.

The Girl Who Teaches Gorillas to Laugh

Cameroon, 2006

The names Dian Fossey and Jane Goodall are emblazoned large in the history of great ape conservation. Fossey's story was immortalised in the Hollywood film *Gorillas in the Mist*, a bittersweet thriller that ends with her brutal murder but became a tour de force in helping focus the world's conscience on the plight of Rwanda's mighty Mountain Gorillas. Dame Jane Goodall is my ultimate hero. In 2009, I had the privilege of receiving an RSPCA animal welfare award at a ceremony where she was guest of honour. Dr Goodall is the world's foremost expert on chimpanzees. She has spent more than 45 years studying their behaviour and championing their protection through groundbreaking projects that help local Africans take charge of the conservation and development of their communities.

In the autumn of 2006, I travelled into the Cameroon rainforest to a meet another woman who deserves a place next to these two great primatologists in the Pantheon of Wildlife Champions. Rachel Hogan is unlike any other person I have met. Brave, self-sacrificing, kind... I ran out of adjectives when I began penning her incredible story. It is the story of a person so committed to the cause of protecting and preserving our closest relatives on the evolutionary tree that she has turned her back on so many of the comforts we take for granted in the 21st century. Her name deserves to be mentioned in the same breath as Fossey and Goodall.

What follows is an abridged account of her fascinating story that I wrote for the *Sunday Express* in the autumn of 2006 under the headline 'The Girl Who Teaches Gorillas to Laugh'.

The sweltering rainforest throbs to the chatter of a million creatures. Buzzing cicadas and raucous parrots create an astonishing surround-sound experience in the muggy, strength-sapping heat. Away from the din, there is one noise that lingers in the heart, if not the ears: the gentle sound of young gorillas and chimpanzees... laughing. The idea that gorillas can see the funny side of life may come as a surprise to those witnessing the barbaric slaughter of these highly intelligent, social and spiritual creatures for the abomination that is the bushmeat trade. A brutal massacre of the chimpanzees and gorillas that inhabit the lowlands of West Africa is taking place because their flesh is regarded as a delicacy. Some of it is even being smuggled for the dining tables of wealthy Europeans. In little more than a decade these magnificent creatures, which share a similar DNA profile with humans, will join the scandalous list of man-made extinctions unless the illegal trade is eradicated. One remarkable British woman is leading the struggle to save the 'orphans' of the forest.

Rachel Hogan is one of the most impressive but unassuming women you could meet. In jeans and sweatshirt deep in Cameroon's rainforest, she is a ceaseless worker helping to raise, nurture and, ultimately, save her precious apes. She is also the woman that makes them laugh. Cuddles and laughter are just part of the therapy Rachel is using as she rescues baby apes and then nurses them back to health, happiness and, perhaps one day, freedom.

When hunters wipe out family groups of gorillas for their meat, the young are left behind to starve or are taken as pets. Often they are suffering from gunshot wounds; almost invariably they are so badly traumatised that they die from broken hearts within a few days. At the headquarters of the Cameroon Wildlife Aid Fund (CWAF) in the Mefou National Park, Rachel runs a rescue operation that has saved the lives of scores of young apes and prepares them for the day when the forests are safe enough for them to be freed. It is a Herculean task, fraught with stress and carried out at an unknown cost to her well-being. Life expectancy in the forests, traditionally known as the White Man's Grave, is little more than 47 years. Rachel has suffered nine malaria attacks and is riddled with a host of parasitic worms and creatures whose life cycles inside the human body would turn most people into screaming wrecks. She earns £150 per month, yet nothing detracts her from organising her team of locally recruited assistants and keepers so that the 1,044-hectare park functions. Often, it means nursing and caring for an individual animal around the clock with the same devotion and attention as its mother.

'Don't think I am some strange white woman who has come to Africa looking for a baby substitute,' is Rachel's opening greeting. The suggestion could not be farther from the truth.

Rachel does not have any veterinary qualifications but years of front-line experience looking after primates are worth a row of letters after her name. Taking her fingers and gently tickling a young gorilla called Shufai under the arms, he lets out the cutest of giggles. Lips curled in a wide, toothy smile, he wriggles, demanding more attention. His laughter gets louder. Like any one-year-old he knows the meaning of love, kindness, security and fun. With Rachel he has them all in abundance.

The guns that killed Shufai's mother and silverback father, along with the rest of his family troop, left him with a shattered arm and even more psychological wounds. Today he is a writhing ball of fun, cuddling Rachel and giggling as she nurses him in her arms.

'It's not all about cuddling, touching them or making them laugh,' says Rachel. 'It's bloody hard work and they will be the death of me. The amount of effort you need to put in 24 hours a day to keep them alive is immense.

'People can look at what we do and say they would love to come here and cuddle the gorillas all day but it's not about that. It's a hard slog caring for them and knowing they rely on you. It's about them, not you.'

Rachel always knew it would be hard graft but working with her beloved apes is a childhood ambition that has come true. While most little girls play with dolls, Rachel had her toy gorillas and chimps. Then, there were family visits to Dudley Zoo to see the gorillas in captivity. After leaving school at 16 Rachel found a job as a factory worker. One day, travelling to work on her motorcycle, she suffered horrific arm injuries in a road crash and was left pondering her future.

'When I was a little girl I always wanted to be a vet but the way things worked out I ended up working in a factory,' she explains. 'Then I had the accident. A car just pulled out in front of my motorbike and I was left badly hurt. I broke both wrists and needed a great deal of surgery. I was 21 and could not work so I started studying and got a place at university.'

But then Rachel saw Michaela Strachan with gorillas on *The Really Wild Show* and became so inspired that she contacted Bristol

Zoo to see if she could work on their project in Cameroon. Within weeks she was taken on as a volunteer.

'I suppose you can say that having the motorbike accident was the luckiest thing that happened to me. After that, everything fell into place and here I am in Africa doing what I always wanted to do with my life.'

Stories like Shufai's are being played out all too frequently in equatorial West Africa. As illegal loggers pillage the forests for precious hardwoods to make furniture for European markets, the bushmeat hunters lurk in the shadows.

With more than 500,000 acres of forest being destroyed annually, the wildest areas where the gorillas survive are becoming increasingly accessible, the apes more vulnerable. In a country with an average wage of £31 a month, the meat from an adult male silverback gorilla can fetch up to £150 a kilogram on the black market. Hunters seek out the profitable adult gorillas and, for the price of a few bullets, will obliterate a family group of a dozen individuals in seconds. It is estimated that 800 lowland gorillas are being slaughtered annually. The babies are left because there is not enough meat on them. Most starve or die from trauma; some are sold on as pets. The lucky ones are rescued by Rachel and her team. Shufai is just one such orphan.

'I have held a baby gorilla which has shown no physical injuries but carries the wounds of having watched its mother, father and whole family group slaughtered before its eyes,' sighs Rachel.

'I have cradled infant gorillas and their eyes are open but they are not seeing anything because they have shut down emotionally. They will look at you as if to say, 'I am not interested in what you are offering. I don't even want you to give me a chance. I just want to die.' I have had one die in my arms and there is nothing you can do.'

At CWAF's Mefou National Park the luckier youngsters are rehabilitated then introduced to other orphans to form new family groups. When they are old enough, they are released into open compounds spread over vast tracts of rainforest within the national park. The electric fences that border each gorilla and chimpanzee troops' domain are a reminder, however, that the forests are still not safe enough for the orphans to be fully free. As long as the hunters can sell bushmeat, each animal has a price on its head. And until they can be freed, Rachel continues to make personal sacrifices to fulfil the role she sees as her raison d'etre.

'If I could have these babies back in the forest with their families I would willingly go back home to Birmingham happy,' she admits. 'As for myself, I don't know if I will ever marry and have children. I go home occasionally and meet my friends and they remind me that I am now in my thirties and ask what I want to do with my life because they are all marrying and settling down. But you have to understand that sometimes there are things in life that are so wrong that it physically hurts if you sit on your backside and do nothing.

'My mum and dad obviously worry about my health, especially the malaria, but such problems are part of the package and my parents know how much the gorillas and chimpanzees mean to me. It's not as if they have had to adapt. They always knew I wanted to work with apes and it was a natural progression when I said I was coming to Cameroon.

'I'm very lucky that I have a close family and have their support, especially that of my mum. When I have a problem with one of the orphans I will call her up for advice. She is a nurse and will suggest this or that.'

'But the simple fact is that the bushmeat trade is increasing. It is no longer about people in villages going out to hunt a chimpanzee or a gorilla for their own families; people are supplying guns, people are putting in money and they are putting orders in for gorillas and chimpanzees. It is a huge business. Today bushmeat is being smuggled out on commercial flights and it has even been found in London and other parts of Europe. A lot of people are doing their best to combat it, but you have to make people aware of the problem. It is a serious conservation issue.'

The days I spent with Rachel were a constant reminder of the hardships the poor of Africa face day-in-day-out and her incredible stoicism in eschewing the luxuries of life in Europe for life in the raw. For one of my nights in the Mefou National Park, bed was a floor in a wooden shed used as a storeroom. It was one of the most memorable night's sleep – or lack of it – in my life. I dared not move under the mosquito net for fear of being confronted, perhaps nibbled, by any one of the incredible creatures scurrying around inches from my head. I swear I awoke during one fitful moment of drowsiness to see the whiskers and beady eye of a scurrying forest rodent. At least it was relatively quiet compared to the bush-babies in the forest canopy that sent shivers down my spine every time they let loose one of their blood-curdling screeches. That fitful night was a good excuse to rise at first light. Birds, apart from the fleeting glimpses of Pin-tailed Whydahs, Little Swifts, Black Kites and countless unidentified doves and parrots I had seen during our drive from the capital, Yaoundé, had remained a tantalising distraction as I interviewed Rachel and her team. With a couple of free hours before we were due to drive back to the city, I set off down one of the forest rides that separated the huge ape enclosures.

Tropical rainforest birding is tough even at dawn. Although the heat and humidity have not built up and most of the blood-sucking insects are slumbering, the birds will not come out to play. Early autumn in Cameroon is too early for the European migrants to have returned, and the resident species are in their post-breeding lull. The forests were all but silent apart from the melancholy calls of the rescued apes. They were too enticing to ignore. I approached a cage where the youngest of the chimpanzees were being nursed and committed the cardinal sin of holding my hand out. One cheeky individual swaggered over and rubbed my palm with his fingers and then held them under his nose. Seconds later, others joined him and completed the rub-and-sniff ceremony. They seemed happy to linger within reach and I gently tickled the back of each of their hairy arms one-by-one. They did not quite laugh but deep in their knowing eyes I could tell they thought of me as a friend.

The temperature began to rise and I sensed the only way to see any birds was sit on my backpack on one of the small tracks between compounds and wait. It proved to be the right tactic. Within seconds, a pied Piping Hornbill perched high on a bare tree in the gorilla enclosure, only to be startled by what I took to be a Fine-spotted Woodpecker that vanished before I could note its field marks. African Thrushes did what thrushes the world over do, scrabbling away in the leaf litter, raising my hopes of something more exotic every time I heard a noise in the undergrowth. From nowhere, an elegant flycatcher materialised, perching precariously on a wispy plant stem that could barely take its weight. Its rusty colour scheme was perfect for a monarch, the flamboyant, long-tailed paradise flycatchers that rank among Africa's most majestic bird families. So close was it, I could see the beautiful texture of its wing feathers and the softness of its smoky, charcoal body feathering. The denim-blue orbital ring that surrounded an inquisitive eye was exactly the same tone as the thin, sharp bill. What species was it? My hefty West African field guide had been too bulky to pack. I did, however, have my trusty reporter's notebook and practiced a lesson learned on that family trip to the Venetian Lagoon years before. I scribbled a matchstick drawing, picking out the relative shortness and shape of its tail and noting the lack of a typical monarch's crest. It would be one to look up when I got back to Britain. If I got back to Britain...

As I was adding the final annotations to my sketch, there was a loud crash of breaking branches and an unearthly grunt in the dense vegetation behind me. I clambered to my feet, my life flashing before as I tried to recall the correct bit of advice on how to escape a mauling. Should I flee, fight, climb a tree, roll into a ball or... I tried to work out a survival strategy but I did not know what kind of creature was homing in on me. Could one of the mature gorillas have escaped their compound? Do elephants roam free in the park? Could it be a big cat? I am no Bear Grylls and most probably chose the worst survival strategy of them all as I tiptoed away, looking over my shoulder and waiting for the monster to emerge. With a final grunt and more thrashing vegetation, the biggest pig I had ever seen marched into the open – the same silvery toned colour as a Hippopotamus and I'd swear it was almost as big – and began snorting the ground totally oblivious to my presence.

Back home, I discovered that the mystery monarch was Bates's Paradise Flycatcher, a little-studied denizen of the forest named after George Latimer Bates, an American naturalist who fell in love with Cameroon. Hopefully, one day the name of Rachel Hogan will be honoured for her contributions to conservation.

The Cameroon Wildlife Aid Fund continues its important work as Ape Action Africa. For more details see www.apeactionafrica.org

The Friendly Heart of Africa
Malawi, 2007

Missing the story is the ultimate sin for any journalist but being scooped by a sharper, more determined rival is an occupational hazard. You win some, you lose some. Failing to dig out the truth through ineptitude, drunkenness or plain apathy on the other hand, well, that's unforgivable. Miss out because you were too busy birding? That's another story...

Malawi features rarely on the travelling birder's itinerary. The country is relatively small – 94,000 square kilometres, compared with neighbouring Zambia's 752,000 – the road networks are relatively good, and in two weeks it is possible to see more than 350 species. However, the paucity of endemics, the large mammals and the long-established safari infrastructure of other African nations mean that globe-trekking birders will usually opt for Kenya, South Africa and Botswana to build their world lists at the expense of this friendly nation. Malawi's boast of being 'the warm heart of Africa' comes with much justification. Bustling, colourful market places are full of smiles; handshakes are friendly and genuine. Many of the tribal rivalries that have so often blighted other African nations with their internecine conflicts, sometimes even full-blown civil wars, have never affected the country that was known as Nyasaland when it was a British protectorate in the early 20th century. With its balmy climate and the natural wonder that is Lake Malawi – the eighth largest lake in the world and home to hundreds of endemic cichlid fish – it is easy to see why this small, endearing nation is anxious to tell the world that it is great place to spend the tourist dollar. Welcoming overseas journalists on fact-finding missions remains one of the best ways to spread the message.

You are never alone in Malawi. At a little more than 12 million its population is two million more than neighbouring Zambia, a nation almost eight times as large, and invariably, even the remotest Malawian roads are heaving with people going about their business. Every journey seems to pass a never-ending stream of children in smart school uniforms walking miles to their classrooms, or women in long skirts and bright cardigans carrying firewood in their hands, vegetables on their heads and babies on their backs. Rickety bicycles from another age are put to good use by workmen and labourers who seem to turn up out of nowhere on the bumpiest stretches of road. Then there are the heaving, open-backed pickups, so overloaded that they make Indian trains look relatively empty, which are used to ferry workers along dusty, rutted tracks. As one may expect, almost every patch of flat land seems to be under cultivation and birds appear to be non-existent.

Drive through the agricultural plains of Spain or Hungary and the fleeting flashes of farmland birds interrupt the journey at reassuring intervals. Travelling south from the relaxed and modern capital of Lilongwe, along bustling roads, I struggled to make out anything that looked like a bird shape let alone an identifiable bird. One of our guides, talking about 'big game', acknowledged mournfully that land pressure meant most of Malawi's large mammals were only found within the safe confines of nature reserves. He could well have said the same about its birds.

After three days of beating the tourist trail to see tea pickers at work in the southern highlands and watch local potteries turn out colourful, rustic ceramics, our party of travel writers and journalists headed for the luxurious Mvuu Camp set on the Shire River, one of Lake Malawi's main outlets and a tributary of the mighty Zambezi. The Shire sounds like something out of *Lord of the Rings* and, indeed, taking a boat trip that first morning on its smooth, inky waters was a truly magical experience. There are more Hippopotamuses lounging and loafing along the Shire – pronounced 'shiray' by the locals – than anywhere else in Africa. Elephants graze the papyrus-lined riverbank and giant Nile Crocodiles lurk below the surface ready to snap at the unwary. Safe within the boundaries of the Liwonde National Park birds abounded, too. Water Thick-knees noisily announced their presence and chequerboard Pied Kingfishers hovered long enough for even the most incompetent of photographers to capture their 'Kodak moments'. The shrill, gull-like calls of African Fish Eagles accompanied the boat as it chugged up and down the river and, for a moment, I had thoughts of Humphrey Bogart's Oscar-winning performance in the classic adaptation of C.S. Forester's thriller. Our own little African Queen docked well away from the nearest lumbering crocodiles and the next stage of our Liwonde adventure was about to begin.

The trip organisers were well aware of my interest in the park's wildlife and arranged a foot safari – accompanied by a guide with a Kalashnikov in case any encounter with the park's fauna became too close. Our walk through sandy scrub scattered with so-called 'fever trees' – acacias that grow close to swampy areas where malaria-carrying mosquitoes flourish – was a colourful introduction to how rich and beautiful Malawi's bird life is when sealed off from the populous outside world by high fences. Endearing Lilian's Lovebirds played lovey-dovey in the branches of a giant Baobab, their flushed faces the colour of bashful teenagers caught in flagrante delicto. Excitable Grey Go-away Birds, a species that I had learned about as a child, screeched their rude dismissals, although I must admit it sounded nothing like 'go away...' Competing with the lovebirds for the title of Malawi's cutest species were the adorable and range-restricted Böhm's Bee-eaters, with their peach-toned crowns and throats and a propensity to dig out their nests in the most inconvenient places, including the middle of sandy tracks. Beautiful paint-by-number birds always hold the attention, but there was one species I was desperate to see – the large, cat-like Pel's Fishing Owl. When field guides, a type of book not known for hyperbole, describe a bird as 'awesome' you know it really is going to be breath-taking. As one would expect with anything awesome, words like elusive and stealthy surely follow. Despite being one of the world's largest owls, the camp's resident bird remained frustratingly invisible during my morning vigil under its favourite roost tree. With the next arrangement on our hectic itinerary beckoning, we enjoyed an excellent brunch in the sumptuous camp surroundings and headed out of the park for a lesson in humility.

Njobvu must be like so many other African villages in the wake of the Aids catastrophe. Children are everywhere, making up 75 per cent of the village's population of 900, as adults succumb to the ravages of a disease very much under control in the affluent West. The absence of grown-ups was the most striking feature as scores of wide-eyed children surrounded our tour bus, screaming and shouting as if we were pop stars or footballers. Grinning boys wearing worn and tawdry hand-me-downs that no British mother would dare put in a charity sack muscled their way into camera shot. Bashful girls lingered in the background.

'That's me! That's me!' Rascally faced youngsters giggled in their Yao language, looking at the multi-million pixel images of themselves on our expensive digital cameras. Atmospheric shots of destitute African children have become something of a cliché for Western journalists to give their readers a tincture of the hardships and travails of the Third World without them having to endure the bitter aftertastes of poverty first hand. My camera clicked and clicked and clicked again. Girls, some barely in their teens, showed the heavy bellies of impending motherhood. Others carried babies on their young, slim shoulders. Older boys looked on apathetically. They had seen the tourist circus before. I sensed their ennui. I had to do something.

Marching over and taking hold of their raggedy football, I ordered them to follow me to the dusty, flat field that doubled up as the village pitch. After dividing the 30 or so bigger lads into two groups, I became the Pied Piper and led the little ones to the sidelines. I threw the ball into the air and, like boys in the back streets of Newcastle or Naples or the favelas of Rio, they began playing the beautiful game. Meanwhile, I began teaching the tots some of their first words of English: come, on, you and Spurs may not help them make their way in this world but hearing them sing out as one as they turned the words into a chant brought a lump to my throat. Their terrace song rang out until two of the bigger boys came together with a sickening thump: think Roy Keane meets Dave McKay.

The ball they had both challenged for collapsed with a sad 'phhhhh!' Ball, perhaps, was a loose word for the bundle of black plastic bags held in place by thin twine that had now sunk into a sad half-moon. I examined it quizzically, wondering how such a ball could bounce and behave like one kicked by two pub teams on a Sunday morning back home. The biggest boy sensed my puzzlement and began to peel away layer after layer of plastic as if it was a Christmas Present. When he got to the core, the reason for the ball's demise became apparent – he pulled out the burst remains of an inflated condom as if he was a magician producing a rabbit out of a hat. Every youngster burst out laughing.

As the joyous sound of children's laughter rang out across the village, one of my fellow travellers was getting to the heart of Njobvu's story. Ciara Leeming is one of the most impressive journalists I have ever worked with, a deep-thinking, writer-photographer whose compassion for life's underdogs flows through her work. Only when I returned back to Britain and read the back story about what was going on in the village in an article she had written for *The Big Issue* did I realise how I had missed so much during the visit during which I spent most of the time organising the ill-fated football match before looking around the surrounding vegetable plots for birds.

Ciara's story revealed how the tensions that once existed between the villagers and the park's rangers over poaching for bushmeat had been slowly eroded by an altruistic desire by safari companies and non-government organisations to ensure the local community felt the benefits of high-end safari tourism. Promoting Njobvu as a 'cultural village' allows tourists to swap safari luxury for a night in a purpose built mud hut, dining on local food and savouring, if that's the right word, African village life in the raw. Those brave souls who had endeavoured came away with rave reviews, while the money they paid for the experience was distributed among the local population through a community fund. At the same time, park workers and a safari company operating a lodge inside Liwonde had helped to build a primary school for 600 children, as many as one in six of them orphans because of Aids.

The spirit of Ciara's article was that conservationists were in a prime position to not only protect and preserve wildlife but also help communities where life expectancy was as low as 38 and where 70 per cent of the population live on less than a dollar a day.

I would like to think that it was being distracted by the impromptu football match rather than compassion fatigue that meant I missed out on the story of Njobvu. For all the children's laughter, there was a haunting realism of how tough life is in rural Malawi, where each day is as much of a struggle for survival as it is for the creatures I had travelled thousands of miles to marvel at. Before we left, one of the boys came up to me with a handmade ball and pressed it into my hands.

'For you,' he said with a smile. I looked down and realised the delicacy of its maker's handiwork. The ball had been wrapped in twine in such a way that it matched the 32-piece patterning of the balls used in the professional game in Europe. Today the ball stands proudly on display in my study, one of my most prized possessions. If only kids in England were prepared to make balls out of recycled plastic bags and played in bare feet. We might win the World Cup again.

That night we had to assemble after dinner for what I had pencilled in as the highlight of the entire tour, the after-dark game drive to see some of the creatures that only became active once the sun sets. Most of the park's predatory mammals are nocturnal and even its large, lumbering herbivores, African Elephant, Hippopotamus and Kudu, were still active in the gloom. The ten-seater, open-top 4x4 with its staggered seats looked perfect for getting a grandstand view, but before we took off into the night one of the guides handed me a hefty spot lamp and led me to the front. Perched above the bull bars was a seat.

'You can be our spotter,' he smiled, giving me the thumbs up. 'It's a great privilege.'

I could not hide my excitement at riding 'shotgun', colouring up in the gloom like a child picked by a teacher to play a leading role in the school nativity. I clambered into the seat, gave the spot lamp a cursory flash and cried out, 'Wagons roll...' The following dispatch later appeared in the *Sunday Express*.

The 4x4 is purring like a contented lion as we bounce along on the ultimate off-road adventure. Headlamps have been dimmed and the only light in the velvety, black sky radiates from a twinkling Venus.

I'm on a night safari in the Liwonde National Park in Malawi, perched like a front-gunner on the bonnet. Rather than a gun I'm clutching a hand-held spotlight with enough candlepower to illuminate Wembley Stadium, and eager to squeeze its trigger switch and light up the inky night that shrouds the movements of another world.

By day, the natural wonder that is camouflage makes many of the shyer creatures of the Malawian bush impossible to see but, by night, the landscape shimmers like the Milky Way above. Nature is acting out its life and death struggles.

The torch beam sweeps through the dark, picking out the shining wings of countless insects and then hits a firmament of green, glowing specks – the reflecting eyes of a vast herd of Impala. Each animal stares unblinking at the light, caught like startled bunnies. Not a single animal reacts. I switch the torch off and we continue on our bumpy journey.

Moments later, the light show begins again. This time the beam picks up the scurrying movements of a spotted cat-like creature, its complex pattern of markings little use in the glare of the spotlight. The whispering aboard the safari vehicle stops; excited eyes stare at the mysterious animal until the guide explains that it is Genet, a rarely seen carnivore. We are lucky. Our luck holds. I detect another shape and fire the beam, this time picking out a smaller but similarly patterned predator with a pointed snout. This time it is a Civet that has abandoned its arboreal haunts to hunt among the thick grass. Cryptic camouflage does nothing to help hide the creature in the glare of the spotlight and, like the Impala moments before, it freezes momentarily, before vanishing into the night with a sweep of its bushy, striped tail.

By now, I'm getting the swing: switch on the beam, scan carefully right to left – I learnt the trick of always scanning binoculars against the direction we read from an artillery officer – and wait for the eyeshine... It's like driving down a road counting cats' eyes, the only difference that we're looking for real, wild cats.

Two bulky Spotted Hyenas suddenly dash across our path. I am shocked by their size as they pass inches from my feet. As I 'beam' them, the light does not catch their eyes but reflects off their huge canine teeth, giant enamel daggers set in the most powerful mammalian jaws on Earth and capable of snapping a human thighbone as if it was a Twiglet. I think I catch a twang of bad breath, the hyenas are that close.

We continue into the night, stopping momentarily to take in a few minutes' star-spotting. I can only make out a few constellations and see that mighty Orion is upside down. Of course, we're in the Southern Hemisphere. I ask the guide to point out the famous Southern Cross but must admit to being hugely underwhelmed. Why do the Aussies get so excited about it? A quick astronomy lesson ensues and we're given an explanation on how to find True South by using a series of pointer stars. The formula is so complicated that I pray I don't ever get lost south of the Equator.

Soon, we're on our way, bounding down a road rutted with tyre tracks. Through a cloud of dust I catch four neon-red lights reflecting the torch beam. I put my hand up to stop the vehicle but the guide is already out and running towards the source of the glow, which is as bright as a car's brake light. He beckons for me to follow.

By the time I am at his side, he is kneeling down. Inches away are two beautifully marked Square-tailed or Mozambique Nightjars, their bark-like patterning providing them with little camouflage as they huddle in the bleached, sandy soil. One touch of the warm ground explains their choice of roost. It's the African winter and I am already wearing a fleece.

Our journey into the night continues. Eyes continue flickering in the dark but many escape our attentions. Have the animals learnt the art of invisibility by simply shutting their eyelids? I decide upon a new tactic and strafe the branches of a large tree with the beam. Wow! Two saucer-sized eyes reflect the beam back in our faces with almost the same intensity. Only an owl, I presume, has retinas large enough to perform such a stunt, but which one? It dawns: Pel's Fishing Owl. The hairs start rising on my neck. My most sought after bird. Our driver has turned the vehicle so that everyone can see into the tree. The bird seems hypnotised. It does not blink once. I try a balancing act, bringing up my binoculars so that I can make out some of the owl's plumage features, but as I do the torch begins to fall from my grip. In the split second it takes to get the beam back on track, the owl must have turned its face or flown off on velvety wings evolved for silent flight. This most of elusive of birds remains elusive. We head off once again.

After a final look at the vast sea of spooky, green-eyed Impala, we head back to camp passing through dense acacia thickets, with me musing that many of the big game hunters who flock to Africa and spend fortunes claiming trophy kills could get their kicks by playing spot-lamper on a night safari – and without shedding any blood. I give a final, cursory sweep of the torch. Four red lights shine back. Nightjars! I wave my hand for the driver to halt and am just about to jump off the bonnet when I realise that I am staring into the devilish, eyes of a pair of Hippopotamus, supposedly Africa's deadliest mammal. All sorts of statistics pinball through my mind: the number of people these powerful herbivores kill each year; the speed a Hippo can run; the length of those incredible lower canines...

We have reached an impasse. The Hippos refuse to budge. The driver thinks about edging forward. Reversing in the dark, forbidding bush is imprudent. If one of these three-ton monsters decides to charge I'm dead. The stand off lasts an age. A call of nature begins to make me feel uncomfortable but no less than the natural wonders confronting us less than 10 feet away. I cross my legs.

Then, a loud, penetrating roar far in the distance breaks the silence, perhaps an obdurate bull elephant or a macho lion. Whatever, the hippos are spooked. They waddle off, wiggling their bottoms comically. Their back views are certainly more reassuring than a face-to-face showdown at a few yards.

We head back to the camp for a nightcap and to celebrate a wonderful evening's communion with the creatures of the Malawian bush. A little more than a century after the famed missionary Dr David Livingstone became the first European to set eyes upon the wonder that is Lake Malawi, I too had made my own exciting discoveries in this, the friendly heart of Africa.

Yet, perhaps, the greatest discovery of all was the realisation that being a tourist is not enough. To help preserve Africa's wildlife and to protect its wildernesses, one needs to ensure that local communities prosper from their natural heritage. Engaging in village projects, laughing and smiling with the people and then making sure that the tourist dollar filters down to the poorest are the best ways to help both humans and fauna and flora alike.

The Longest Drive
California, 2001

The distance between the old mining town of Lee Vining and the breaking surf of Monterey Bay is exactly 180 miles. Put in twitching terms, the mileage is identical to the journey from London to Liverpool, a drive most self-respecting bird listers can do in their sleep to secure a decent tick. While the Thames–Mersey run is nothing more than a four-hour jaunt along unprepossessing slabs of motorway, the day-long odyssey from the shores of Mono Lake to the sight of those impressive Pacific breakers is a trail blaze in the spirit of the '49ers, the gold prospecting pioneers that opened the West's last frontier.

The temperature gauge on the tour bus was hovering just above freezing as I looked out over Mono's calm, salty waters with such stirring memories. For three days, the tour group I was leading for a British holiday company had birded the sage brush and crystallized margins of America's oldest body of open water, created by powerful volcanic forces 750,000 years ago and almost destroyed during the Seventies. Attempts to draw Mono's drainage basin to supply Los Angeles' burgeoning population saw the water level plunge, exposing the lake's unique California Gull colony to coyote predation and igniting one of the most famous environmental lawsuits in history.

Conservationists won the day, water levels began to rise and Mono's unique ecosystem was saved. A combination of hypersalinity – it has been estimated that the lake contains 280 million tons of dissolved salts – and a high alkalinity has seen endemic brine shrimps evolve in the murky waters to bolster a food chain topped by vast numbers of migratory birds dependent on the abundant protein to fuel their seasonal journeys. An estimated two million birds rest and feed here during the course of the year, the vast majority Black-necked Grebes and Red-necked and Wilson's Phalaropes. Looking out with a scope at a carpet of phalaropes spinning alongside 'tufa towers' – elaborate soda lake structures that look like giant wedding cakes – had been one of the many memorable moments of a tour that was spanning the length and breadth of America's most diverse state. They say that California is a continent on its own and, as we headed west, the next twelve hours would prove just that.

Lee Vining had certainly proved to be a luckier place to stay than it had for the old gold rush prospector who had given his name to this outpost on the eastern slopes of the Sierra Nevada. The original Leroy Vining founded the town as a mining camp during the 1852 gold rush but somehow he shot himself accidentally before he could find his fortune. His name lives on as the town has become a popular base for birders wanting to explore both Mono Lake and the nearby freshwater and equally 'birdy' Crowley Lake as well as the alkaline flats that play host to some of America's more restricted and sought after species such as both Sage and Brewer's Sparrows and the beautiful and elusive Greater Sage-Grouse. Besides attracting birders, Lee Vining is also a popular stop-off for tourists heading towards one of America's great wildernesses – Yosemite National Park.

America loves hyperbole, especially when it is used to sell something. The PR slug for Yosemite is a piece of lyrical mastery: 'Not just a great valley... but a shrine to human foresight, strength of granite, power of glaciers, the persistence of life, and the tranquillity of the High Sierra.' Our journey that cool, late September morning would take us across the entire breadth of a park that covers 1,200 square miles of forest and mountain and was first preserved under an 1864 bill signed by Abraham Lincoln at the height of the American Civil War. Almost 120 years later, the park was designated a World Heritage Site and today it attracts 3.7 million visitors per year. Most squeeze themselves into the compact, bustling, some may say over-commercialised, Yosemite Village with its cafe, grill, souvenir shops and visitors' centre. More intrepid spirits are prepared to explore the wilder reaches.

Leaving Lee Vining with a frost on the ground and the vehicle's temperature gauge touching 32 °F (0 °C), we headed towards the park's easternmost gate, Tioga Pass, climbing a precipitous gradient that left our tour bus wheezing as it went from 6,300 feet above sea level to 9,943 feet in little less than half an hour. It wasn't only the bus gasping for breath. My lungs tightened with the drop in oxygen levels as I jumped out to take a few atmospheric photographs of the first fluttery flakes of autumn snow descending on Lake Tioga. The temperature had plunged to 28 °F (-2.2 °C) too cold for me, still in a summer shirt and shorts, but not for the flocks of powdery blue Pinyon Jays that were scavenging among the treetops. Unlike the other blue jays we had been watching earlier in the tour – Western

Scrub and Steller's – the Pinyon Jays had much smaller tails and a nutcracker-like bill, perfect for winkling seeds out of Pinyon Pine cones. This small jay is hailed as one of the great examples of convergent evolution, mirroring the attributes of nutcrackers to eke out a living in a habitat where pine cones provide the only source of food.

To emphasise the point, as the jays moved through the trees, the beautiful pearl grey form of a Clark's Nutcracker flapped into view on black-and-white wings and set about destroying a pine cone and filling its chin or 'sublingual pouch' – an elasticated sac capable of storing up to 100 seeds at a time – patently aware that winter had arrived. So it had. The cold forced us to hurriedly return to the warmth of the bus to continue our journey west. Over the previous week, our tour group had also stayed on the western side of Yosemite, rubbing shoulders with the late-season vacationers in their giant Winnebagos and marvelling at the breathtaking natural wonders of El Capitan – the 3,000-foot sheer rock face that has become a favourite for climbers and BASE jumpers – and the equally impressive Half Dome, a giant, granite pinnacle that glows red at sunset. The park holds birds aplenty, too. Brown Dipper, Townsend's Solitaire, Mountain Chickadee and the astonishing Red-breasted Sapsucker, a small woodpecker that looks as if its head and chest have been dipped like a French fry in tomato ketchup, had all found their way on the group checklist.

Repeated attempts to find the resident Great Grey Owl had been thwarted by the previous summer's forest fire, which had driven it from a stakeout I had been given, but the trees were alive with migrating wood-warblers, flitting and zipping through leafy, lichen-covered canopy. One morning, our group had patiently waited under the protective branches of a large conifer as the rains came down and we were rewarded with a warbler firework display. Adjectives fail to do justice to the mixed flock of warblers that exploded under skies turning from grey to milky blue which, perhaps, explains why those who named these arboreal sprites opted to immortalise naturalists rather than celebrate their plumage features. Hence, we were treated to stunning views of Audubon's, Townsend's and Wilson's Warblers rather than 'Yellow-throated-yellow-rumped Warbler', 'Black-streaked-golden Warbler' and 'Black-crowned-brilliant-yellow Warbler'. I guess field guide publishers were happy not to run out of ink printing such sesquipedalian monikers. The mixed flock did hold one western warbler rather conservatively named for its plumage, the Black-throated Grey Warbler, along with Hermit Warbler (surely it should be 'Golden-faced Warbler'), Cassin's Vireo and a trumpeting Red-breasted Nuthatch, a species that had delighted one of the biggest twitches in British history a few autumns earlier at Holkham Meals, Norfolk. The fleeting glimpses I still pictured from that occasion were blown away by the tiny male, a striking contrast of slate-grey and cinnamon and a thick supercilium that looked like it had been squirted out from a toothpaste tube. It came within touching distance while it worked along a low branch, all the time heralding its presence with a fanfare of squeaky, trumpeting calls.

There was only time for the briefest of stops on the return journey to look once more for the Great Grey Owl among a stand of long-dead pine trees. Our schedule was tight and the bird appeared to have moved on to new territory. We needed to move on to new territory, too, and continue our descent out of the Yosemite massif and past the impressive Giant Sequoia groves at Tuolumne where, earlier in the tour, we had marvelled at the tiny cones that germinate into trees that can grow almost as tall as the 360-foot dome of St Paul's Cathedral during their 2,500-year lifespan.

The road west followed the course of the fast-running, boulder-laden Merced River with its Common Mergansers (the American race of our own Goosander) and Brown Dippers. A Mountain

Quail, a stubby game bird with striped flanks and a preposterous headdress made up of a single plume that rises at least four inches perpendicularly from the bird's crown and gives the impression of a young Native American brave, had been a popular attraction with the tour party days before. I slowed instinctively, hoping to catch sight of the bird again, only for loud shouts from the back to ring out and order me to stop. Someone had spotted a bear cub on the other side of river. Within seconds, everyone was picking up their cameras and trying to focus on the youngster as it wandered aimlessly across a hillside stripped down by an earlier forest fire. The youngster was sniffing the air anxiously and appeared to be calling. A few moments later we were to find out why it was so fretful.

Having caused a jam – scores of other drivers were stopping to get photographs of the cub – I thought it best to hurry our party along so that we could continue our journey. Back in the coach, I had only driven for a few seconds when the reason for the cub's distress became obvious. On the other side of the river, no more than 50 yards away, a female Black Bear with another cub in tow was beating a hurried path towards her lost offspring. A disaster loomed. Between the three bears, a tourist family had just added the finishing touches to their camp for the night. A picnic table was set in front of a spacious luxury tent and camp chairs were carefully positioned around a flickering campfire. Cool boxes and, ironically, what looked like bear-proof food containers were piled up ready for a sumptuous family picnic. I pulled up and jumped from the vehicle sensing a catastrophe. Others followed, calling out to the campers to warn that a huge sow bear was, literally, bearing down on them.

The American Black bear may be the smallest ursine and far less dangerous than the powerful Grizzly, but a 200 lb female separated from her cub is one mean beast; each year two or three people end up being mauled and eaten by one.

There was nothing cute or cuddly about the bear that was now 50 paces from the camp and closing in fast. Cars were pulling over. Screams were hurled across the Merced at the unsuspecting campers.

'Bear! Bear! There's a bear heading your way!' screamed one terrified middle-aged woman.

'Get over this side of the river quick,' shouted her husband, pointing towards the muscular beast that had paced out another few steps. The animal was now on to a scent and moving fast.

'The bear's just upstream. You haven't much time.'

I tried to urge caution about screaming out. Waving to warn the family was one thing, shouting could alarm the animal. Bears have poor sight but their hearing and sense of smell are as acute as any predator. A shrill noise could panic the mother bear with disastrous consequences. Tension had reached the point where some women in the ever-growing crowd were beginning to cry.

A woman and child, perhaps as young as three, emerged from the camp and began wading through the fast-flowing but fortunately shallow waters. Terror was etched on the woman's face as she clutched her daughter's hand making sure the child did not stumble on the slippery boulders. Behind her stood the husband holding a baby, one hand gripping the child close to his chest, the other urging the woman to carry on to our side of the river. By now, the bear had entered the camp and was sniffing a cool box while the man squatted on his haunches on the other side of the tent, creating a protective shield for his baby. Someone spoke about getting their gun, others were calling the 911 emergency line. The moment the woman reached our side of the river, people clambered down the slope from the road to comfort her. She looked distraught. Her husband was still hiding behind the tent, realising that the bear would pull him down in a few strides if he tried to dash across the ten yards of river bubbling river.

Now we could only watch. Some men talked about wading across the river to frighten the bear away with stones and sticks, others urged caution. The bear had given up on the food containers. She returned to sniffing the air for scent. We prayed she would sense her cub rather than the terrified man and his baby. Then, something else caught her eye.

She moved towards the camp chairs and we could see her bare, fleshy snout twitching as she detected the traces of human scent. Her cub watched intently. Then, in act of pure comedy genius, the bear stood up and parked her somewhat broad posterior down on the green canvas chair as if collapsing into a seat after a hard day at the office. For two or three seconds the chair held her weight and then, with an audible snap, it collapsed, the bear landed on her backside and looked positively startled, perhaps even embarrassed. She sat for an age on the ground, the shattered remnants of the chair under her bulk. On our side of the river, the tension lifted in an instant. There was a spontaneous burst of laughter. Someone clapped. The bear's acute hearing caught the commotion and she began running away from the camp, thankfully in the direction of her lost cub, which could be seen on a slope in the distance. People were still laughing. The father had headed in the opposite direction to the bear and was beginning to ford the river downstream. I wish I had brought a video camera. Jeremy Beadle would have paid handsomely for such comic footage.

The drama over, we continued the drive westwards, the vehicle's temperature gauge had reached a comfortable 70 °F and the Tioga Pass snow clouds had been left far behind. Fast-running streams and hillsides coated with uniform pines slowly gave way to cowboy country with its rolling parkland of sun-bleached grass dotted with evergreen oaks. Turkey Vultures soared overhead on dihedral wings. Every radio channel seemed to be playing Middle America's two favourite types of music – country and western.

With the cruise control set on a legal 50 mph – we had seen plenty of Californian Highway patrolmen secreted off road, powerful motorcycles ticking over – and the air conditioning dial going up at increasing intervals, I chewed up the miles along a laser beam of a road. Either side, a monotonous landscape of irrigated fields growing anonymous crops stretched as far as the eye could see. There were no clouds to break up the pristine blue sky and the uniformity reminded me of the revolving backgrounds used in children's cartoons: telegraph pole, irrigation ditch, homestead... telegraph pole, irrigation ditch, homestead... Only the readings on the temperature gauge and the mileage on the odometer were changing – both were rising by the minute.

California's Central Valley is so vast that it could almost swallow up West Virginia. Once a dry, semi-desert, the valley's 22,000 square miles are now so fertile they amount to one per cent of American land under cultivation but produce more than eight per cent of its agricultural output, worth more than $17 billion to the economy. The conversion from arid wilderness to prime farmland is a feat of engineering mastery, with an irrigation system controlling the river system to prevent flooding one season and supplying precious water during the long, dry periods produced by the hot Mediterranean climate.

We seemed to be driving during the hottest time of the year. By mid-afternoon, the onboard thermometer was showing 106 °F. We had been on the road for seven hours, had descended 10,000 feet from the high-altitude Tioga Pass to an agricultural plain a few feet above sea level and experienced a temperate range of almost 80 degrees. I decided not work out the miles we had travelled. Mental arithmetic is the easiest way to lose concentration on the road and allow the mind to surrender to the seductive charms of drooping eyelids. A flutter of white wings provided enough adrenalin to sweep away the road weariness.

Spotting a party of Cattle Egrets near Fresno was a lesson in one of the most dynamic range expansions of any bird in history. In the Thirties, the vanguard of the egret invasion made landfall in the Americas when a number of African birds crossed the Atlantic and settled in Suriname. Within a decade, they were breeding in Florida. Another decade and they had reached New Jersey to the north and Texas to the west. A species that many thought was most at home scavenging insects at the feet of elephants was now reaching the cattle lands of the Midwest. By the turn of the millennium, they were within a few beats from the Pacific and providing a fillip for long-distance drivers.

The egrets well in our wake, the seemingly endless stretch of straight road at last started meandering. There were ripples in the topography. Distant hills loomed on the horizon. For 60 miles we had driven in a straight line across chequerboard-patterned farmland; now oak trees began to appear at increasing intervals. Yellow grasslands glowed gold in the afternoon light. The relentless blue sky became pitted with the shapes of circling raptor wings. Red-tailed Hawks soared high and White-tailed Kites hovered on fast beating moth-like wings. Ubiquitous Turkey Vultures remained, well, ubiquitous.

One farmstead looked perfect for a roadside leg-stretch and a check for one of California's marquee birds. I set up my scope and, within seconds, the unmistakable shape of undoubtedly my most troublesome bird at home came into focus – a magpie. Trying to justify their nest-raiding antics to children who have just buried a brutalised baby Blackbird does little for the bird's reputation or mine. I must have received more letters from irate readers about the 'Magpie Problem' than any other subject. Attempts at explaining that these intelligent corvids survive by feeding their fledglings other birds' young invariably degenerates from a tempered discussion about the natural order into calls for widespread persecution. I try to keep quiet on the subject these days. Not this day, though. As the magpie shifted its position, I let out a loud 'got it' and hurriedly put the members of the tour group on to a bird with one of the most restricted ranges in America – the Yellow-billed Magpie. There was no question of picaphobia, if that's what you call a pathological hatred of magpies. Everyone was transfixed by the banana-yellow tones of its bill and the tiny flaps of skin under the eyes. Someone even accepted they would willingly swap their despised resident European birds for one of these dandies.

Almost ten hours and 282 miles after we had set off from Lee Vining with snow in the air and mountain birds on our minds, the Pacific was glistening before us in the early evening light. California and Western Gulls provided an escort as we navigated through the streets of Monterey, a town not only enshrined in American literature by John Steinbeck's classic novel *Cannery Row* but also in birding folklore as the base of some of the best pelagic cruises anywhere. This was to be our base for the next leg of the tour. There was still time for one more drama.

Describing how many life zones we had passed during the 10,000 foot descent from the high Sierra to the Pacific shoreline would have challenged a top-grade biology student. There were six biomes in Yosemite alone, ranging from the Arctic-Alpine slopes with stunted Red Mountain Heather, Rock Fringe, Alpine Gentian and Steer's Head to the deciduous Freemont Cottonwood Trees of the park's lower levels. Now, at Pacific Grove, a residential suburb of Monterey, we were watching Black Oystercatchers, Black Turnstones and Surfbirds working the rockpools of a rugged shoreline draped with kelp fronds. And there was still more biodiversity to observe. As we walked back to the tour bus I noticed what looked like a discarded inner tube coiled in the road. Closer inspection revealed it was a snake, maybe two feet long, beautifully marked with black, yellow and red linear stripes, and seemingly unharmed despite its resting place on the warm concrete surface heavily marked with burnt rubber. I knelt down to see if the reptile was alive and a lithe tongue poked out, sensing my presence. I jumped back. I had previous history with serpents.

A few years before, I had been on a birding trip in Florida when the dangers – and inconveniences – caused by close encounters with snakes taught me a lasting lesson about these beautiful reptiles. They can be obdurate blighters! On that occasion, I had been birding in the National Audubon Society's impressive Corkscrew Swamp Sanctuary and had followed the two-mile boardwalk trail that gives visitors a unique view of the heart of the otherwise impenetrable cypress forest with its sultry atmosphere and trees decorated with ferns and bromeliads. This was the home of the remarkable Limpkin, a bird that combines the skeletal features of a crane with the behaviour of a crake and possesses a long, ibis-like bill adept at dealing with the prey item that dominates its diet, large Apple Snails. For more than two hours I had absorbed the swamp's sights and sounds as I pounded the springy wooden boardwalk and sweated in the muggy humidity. My calves were already celebrating as I approached the last few planks of the trail when I was confronted by a large, black snake stretched out across my path. Before I could take a step, the creature reared up and opened its mouth, exposing fearsome fangs set in a mouth which looked like fluffy white clouds – it was the notorious Cottonmouth or Water Moccasin, a snake whose aggressive nature and deadly bite has featured in many a cowboy B-movie, invariably with deadly consequences for the bad guys.

From what I could remember, Cottonmouths move quickly on land and water and take unkindly to being disturbed. I had two choices: walk two miles back the way I came or make the snake move from its suntrap. Tiredness rather than courage held sway. I approached the snake with the legs of my tripod stretched out.

Crocodile Hunter Steve Irwin had only just reached British television screens with his snake-catching antics. Any idea of emulating him ended the second the snake reared once more and showed off its inch-long fangs and more of its menacing white mouth. I froze. Another tactic was required. I looked for something to throw but there were no stones or sticks on the boardwalk. I tried bouncing on the boards but the snake's obstinacy knew no bounds. I turned and, within two strides of turning my back, there was a sound of something plopping into the water. One look over my shoulder revealed the snake had slithered off the path and into the oily-black waters. What had frightened it away I will never know, but above Corkscrew Swamp a Red-shouldered Hawk was casting an intimidating shadow.

Now, looking down at a snake coiled on the busy coast road and remembering how the Cottonmouth had been spooked by a shadow, I tried waving my arms like a hawk to make it move. No luck. I tried the gentle art of persuasion, impersonating Steve Irwin in my best Australian.

'Come 'ere, li'l fella, you don't wanna get run over now, do ya?' The snake looked at me the same way the children used to when I tried my comedy impressions at home.

It was time for measured force. I extended the leg of my tripod and gently hooked it under the snake's belly, planning to lift and dunk it on to the verge in one movement. The snake had different thoughts. Halfway through the delicate procedure, it began to coil around the leg like a quick-growing vine. Three firm shakes failed to budge it. Positive action was required. I lifted the tripod and made a fast grab for the animal's tail. It was faster. The instant I touched its scaly skin, the snake was sinking its fangs into my wrist.

I screamed, anticipating the red-hot pain of a snakebite followed by some nasty necrotising venom that would have my arm withering and dropping off within the hour. Yet all I could feel was two faint pinpricks. I looked down and the snake was wrestling to bite through the cuff of my fleece. I took two steps, shook my arm and the snake dropped on to the verge and then slithered away. I slithered away, too. Proud that I had joined the ranks of intrepid adventurers and explorers who had faced the threat of a snake bite, but somewhat embarrassed that I had been petrified by a creature that could hardly savage a piece of clothing. Later that night, I looked up its description and discovered I had been attacked by a Garter Snake, perhaps even the extremely rare San Francisco Garter Snake, one of America's most endangered reptiles, and described as 'harmless to humans'. Harmless? It almost had my arm off.

Howler

Arizona, 2003

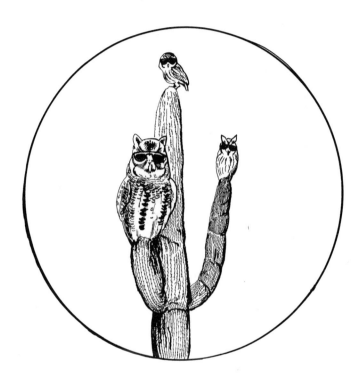

The ghost of Geronimo hovered on the warm breeze of a new day. Deep in the Chiricahua Mountains, where the great warrior's Apache nation had fought a long and bloody war against the US Cavalry, the mournful strains of Native American pipe music were echoing off red stone formations and being carried along on the ripples of fast-running stream water. Exactly where these atmospheric sounds were emanating from in such a remote outpost as Cave Creek Canyon, I never found out, but the music, like the birds I saw that day, live forever in my memory.

Arizona is as attractive a destination for today's birders as it was to those early pioneers of the 1880s who were drawn to the desert by the lure of silver and gold and cattle country. The gunfight at the OK Corral and the killing of Billy the Kid are just two of the legendary adventures that were played out across the arid landscape, but it was Geronimo's guerrilla tactics against the cream of the US Cavalry that led to the warrior become one of the Wild West's most enduring figures. Walking in the shadowy canyon that warm April morning, with the lilting Apache pipes harmonising with birdsong, one could imagine the fear and trepidation of a suppressed people knowing that invaders wanted to clear them from the incomparably beautiful lands of their ancestors. For all the uncompromising harshness of the mesquite desert that envelopes the Chiricahuas, deep inside the mountain range sweetwater springs burst forth supporting so-called 'sky islands' – biodiversity-rich enclaves – where some of America's rarest birds and mammals survive.

The Chiricahua range, which sweeps up 3,000 feet from a desert floor that is already 3,000 feet above sea level, is the continuation of a Mexican range and acts as a conduit for several Central American species to reach US soil. Take a look at the Sibley field guide and every few pages there are range maps for a species such as Grey Hawk or Violet-crowned Hummingbird which show that they are only found in North America in this remote south-west corner of Arizona.

The same goes for some of America's rarest mammals. Jaguar and Ocelot used to breed in the mountains and have both supposedly been seen in recent times. With a bird list of around 375, numerous national rarities and spellbinding scenery, Arizona has become one of the hottest birding destinations for not only fanatical American listers but overseas travellers, too. It has also attracted some of the top birders around to act as guides.

'Call me Bob,' beamed a giant figure as huge as a gridiron defensive linesman with a smile as broad as his wide shoulders. 'I'm your guide for the day.'

From that moment, and in deference to a certain children's television show, our guide instantly became 'Bob the Birder'. And what a birder! Knowing your local patch is a prerequisite for anyone who wants to charge visitors for showing them around, but when it comes to meeting the expectations of demanding birders and showing them the rarest and most elusive species in the toughest of habitats, it takes great field skills, stamina and plenty of hard work. Within minutes of Bob climbing aboard our tour vehicle, you could see he was a birder's birder; his eyes constantly alert and on the prowl while holding conversation. Every flutter of bird wings and every fleeting flypast caught his attention as we headed out from the small village of Portal towards the desert scrub that skirts the Arizona–New Mexico state border. Almost as soon as we climbed from the vehicle, Bob was pointing out two of the desert's most wanted specialities: Bendire's and Crissal Thrashers, bizarre, highly secretive birds that use their down-curved bills to probe for insects and spiders that lurk in the sparse patches of vegetation.

They reminded me somewhat of Hoopoe Larks I had seen years before in Israel's Negev, playing coy for long periods and then producing the most atmospheric songs to bring life to the barren terrain. The Crissal Thrasher was far more striking than the nondescript Bendire's; its bill was longer and far more decurved, and a rusty vent was easy to detect even in the dawn light. Rather than perform a spectacular song-flight, the thrasher seemed happy to climb atop a dead branch to deliver a series of fluty, melodic notes that only added to its charisma. From nowhere, a covey of Scaled Quail, delicate game birds with a scallop-patterned plumage seemingly crafted by goldsmiths, ran like excited nuns across our path before vanishing back into the scrub. Overhead, a pair of Swainson's Hawks had achieved enough uplift in the cool, dawn air to begin patrolling their territory; the thrashers went coy. Bob's itinerary was running like clockwork.

The lure of Arizona, particularly its historical place in the opening of the Wild West, the array of incredible geographical features and its knack of attracting rare Mexican birds into the 'Lower 48', had made the state my number one destination ever since I had begun building up a North American list. By the spring of 2003, the tally was already edging towards the 600 mark, a reasonable figure even by American birding standards and, pro rata, significantly more impressive than my British list which, to this day, still has many glaring omissions.

When I was asked to team up with an old friend and veteran tour leader Peter Dedicoat to help him on a state-wide odyssey that snaked from Phoenix down to the Mexican border and then north again as far as the Grand Canyon, I was packed and at the check-in almost instantly. Along the way, we would be meeting up with several local specialists who would help us to see some of America's rarest and most highly sought specialities. Bob the Birder was the guide who would be taking us into the inner sanctum of Geronimo's domain, where only 120 years earlier no European would dare venture.

My diary takes up some of the story:

If there was one place that Geronimo would have felt safe in his long war with the US Cavalry then it would have been Cave Creek Canyon, with its towering red stone rock formations, running streams and thick, impenetrable woodland dominated by lush Arizona Sycamore. As the tour group arrived, the soft strains of Native American pipe music filled the air. Where it came from, I never found out, but the sounds mixed with the dawn chorus created a perfect atmosphere for birding in Apache country, and soon we were sampling its most famous specialities. Painted Redstart, a glorious monochrome bird with a fiery red belly, played coy for several minutes deep in the riparian forest before breaking into the open and fanning its black-and-white tail. Redstart actually means red tail but there were no 'goods descriptions' complaints about this dandy of a bird.

Other South o' the Border specialities followed aplenty. Mexican Jay, a uniformed cobalt blue jay closely related to the commoner Scrub Jay and with two distinct populations here in Arizona and another in Texas, followed hot after the redstart. Moments later we were looking at a bird with an even more restricted range. Arizona Woodpecker has chosen a brown and white colour scheme rather than the pied uniform of many of its Picoides' relatives such as Downy and Hairy Woodpeckers, and by doing so has made it even more difficult to pick out as it shinned up trunks the same chocolate tones as its mantle. Only the vermilion flash of the male's nape helped me get a binocular view before it evaporated into the canopy.

Each step deeper into the canyon seemed to produce new birds. A Greater Pewee with the subtlest of crests, more of a topknot really, sallied back and forth across the track that led ever deeper into the canyon. Bob's sharp eyes picked out a Hepatic Tanager the colour of raw liver perched high in a sycamore and close by two recent splits – Plumbeous and Cassin's Vireo – were seen close together, perhaps justification for the authorities separating them from the previous umbrella name of Solitary Vireo!

The Apache music faded as the sun's warming rays invaded the valley floor, only to be replaced by sounds that were to herald one of the highlights of the tour – a soft, almost dog-like yelping which was transformed into the brilliant greens and bubblegum pinks of an Elegant Trogon. Elegant is just too poor an adjective for this mind-blowing concoction that reminds you of a nightclub cocktail more than a bird. Fortunately, for short periods it would perch solemnly in dense foliage, incredibly well protected from prying eyes even though its chest and belly are about as bright a colour scheme as was ever adopted by any living creature.

Bob's knowledge of Apache country is not confined to finding great birds; it also extends to turning up excellent picnic spots. Lunch was taken in the grounds of the South Western Research Station, an academic base for biologists, geologists and anthropologists studying the riches of the Chiricahuas and set in wooded grounds with a wonderful backdrop of impressive mountain scenery. As if by magic, Bob's ears soon picked up the plaintive whistles of a Northern Pygmy Owl, a tiny terrier of a bird that most probably punches more above its weight than any other predator. From deep within a juniper overlooking the car park, the distinctive soft whistles seemed to get increasingly louder but seeing this well-camouflaged, sparrow-sized creature was an altogether harder challenge. After much searching, and several false calls that turned out to be nothing more than twisted branches, the owl finally surrendered itself by moving onto to an exposed snag and began blinking nonchalantly in the daylight unaware of the attention it was getting.

The afternoon saw us visiting a drier area of woodland for one of the region's most elusive species: Buff-breasted Flycatcher, a tiny 'Empid' with highly specialised habitat requirements – arid pine clearings. With Bob the Birder's local knowledge and excellent hearing, we were soon looking at this striking little bird with its gingery underparts and strong wing-bars. The forest area was to produce one further surprise. From out of nowhere a pair of Montezuma Quail – the male highly speckled and with a melancholy face that looks as if it has been stained with tear-drops, his mate a far dowdier individual – appeared suddenly and proceeded to trundle along a path before settling momentarily in a small clearing, providing views few Americans witness in a lifetime's birding.

The Cave Canyon experience ranks up there with my finest days' birding anywhere. Every other tree seemed to deliver a new bird but even the most myopic of listers could not fail to have been consumed by the atmosphere that, for all its association with the brutal Apache Wars, exuded peace and tranquillity. Countless cinematic productions may have painted Geronimo and Cochise as nothing more than barbaric savages but the Apache were deeply spiritual people in harmony with the mountains, forest and deserts:territory they loved and were not prepared to surrender without a fight.

After the day's exertions, the group headed back to our base at Portal for a late siesta or a chance to inspect the hummingbird feeders that decorate virtually every garden in this tiny hamlet. Main Street Portal amounts to nothing more than a general store, post office and a half dozen or so front gardens, each decked out with a variety of hummingbird feeders that seemed to be constantly buzzing with the sound of wingbeats. Whatever a feeder's colour or design, each seemed to be attended by flashing sprites that would appear from nowhere to fill up with sugar water and then vanish within a blink of an eye. That said, we were able to watch the comings-and-goings of five emerald jewels – Broad-billed, Blue-throated, Magnificent, Black-chinned and Broad-tailed Hummingbirds – from the comfort of a bench strategically placed below one garden's hummer feeding station.

There's nothing like watching others working to recharge the batteries and no creature works quite as hard as a hummingbird with a thirst for nectar or sugar-water. An hour's entertainment at the feeders had revitalised the tour group in time for Bob's famous finale – the so-called 'owl prowl'. Pinning down owls for travelling birders keeps bird guides busy from the Arctic to the tropics. Finnish and Central European birders spend the harsh winter months locating nest holes ready for the spring onslaught of those who are prepared to pay handsomely for the sight of a Great Grey, Ural, Hawk or

Tengmalm's Owl. The forests of Arizona can be as bountiful as those in Europe. Bob had been busy over the past few weeks.

Before we set off under a setting sun, Bob gave us a few words of caution 'Keep close,' he warned in the stern tones that Americans do so well. 'I don't carry a gun and I've only got firecrackers in my pocket. Up in those hills there are bears and cougars. Some of them may even be rabid. You don't want to come across a cougar in the dark and you certainly don't want to come across one that has rabies.'

There was a collective gulp.

I had already ridden my luck on that tour. Arizona is 'rattler country'. Thirteen species exist with names as frightening as their bite. Sidewinders and the exotic Massasauga, the Tiger Rattlesnake and the infamous Western Diamond-backed are primed and lurking under rocks or dry leaf litter ready to inject their excruciating venom into the unwary. The first rattler to confront us during the tour had been a four-foot Black-tailed Rattlesnake that had been happy to slide away as soon as it felt the vibrations of our footsteps. But next time...

Birding may focus the eyes and heighten the hearing, but common sense invariably vanishes in the heat of the moment when every sense is honed on finding birds. Walking along a desert trail, I had dismissed the buzzing noise at my feet as nothing more than an overactive bee on pollen-collecting duties. I was intent on getting some crisp video footage of a male Pyrrhuloxia, the desert version of the Northern Cardinal, perched on a cactus top. It was playing coy. Getting the right angle to capture the bird's rosy-red neck tie and its pointed Mohican 'war brave' headdress meant I was jigging around like a camp-fire dancer and kicking up enough dust to send a smoke signal. The buzzing continued but I followed the advice I had given my children many times: never over react when a bee's about because it does not want to hurt you. As soon as the Pyrrhuloxia got bored of the photo-shoot and flew out of view, I pressed the stop button on the camera and went to put it my backpack, looking down on the ground to avoid stamping on the bee. There, looking up at me was the tiniest of rattlers, no more than a foot long, mouth wide open and shaking its tail as if it was playing the maracas. Perhaps the amount of dust I had kicked up had prevented it from moving off. It looked cute enough to pick up for closer inspection but something told me to leave well alone...

Hours later, when I regaled the story to a barfly back at the hotel, he looked at me as if I was mad.

'Ya nearly picked the li'l critter up?' He asked, sucking in a deep breath and shaking his head. 'No one ever told ya that a baby rattler is born with enough venom to put a mule on its back? They're not cute, they're killers.

How big d'ya say it was?'

I measured 12 or so inches with my hand.

'That was a year-old snake – amazing that he never bit home. Y'sure wouldn't be here now, if he had.'

I never waited around to find out if he meant 'here', as in the hotel bar, or simply still alive.

With Bob's cautionary words about rabid bears, coyotes and cougars and enough snake encounters under my belt to make an Animal Planet documentary, we drove back towards Cave Creek, the sun enhancing the rich red tones of the Chiricahuas. We were about to prowl for owls.

My diary takes up the story:

Bob's local knowledge and preparation, once again paid dividends as we left Portal. En route for the canyon, we detoured into open country and our first stop for the evening.

Timing was critical, Bob explained. We were heading for an Elf Owl nest and had to arrive as the bird was leaving the sanctuary of its daytime roost to hunt the desert for insects. Elf Owl is the smallest owl in the world, 5.5 inches long and 1.4 oz, according to my Sibley field guide. There was barely enough light left in the day for the bird to be seen as it emerged from the nest hole, widened its cat-like amber-and-black eyes and then disappeared on silent wings. The whole performance lasted less than 10 seconds but another of Arizona's star attractions had obliged us with its grace. We tiptoed away silently; Bob's warning about mountain predators was still fresh in our minds.

Within minutes, Bob was leading the way to another stakeout. This time, we were on the trail of Western Screech-Owl. Bob knew a nest site and, there, true to his word, a small 'eared owl', again with hypnotic feline eyes, blinked in the gloom, its dark streaked breast perfect camouflage for woodland haunts. The much rarer Whiskered Screech-Owl, a species that just about makes it over the border from Mexico, was the next on our nocturnal jaunt and was duly delivered by Bob with similar aplomb, using the same pack drill of silent approach and careful listening, although I would be the first to admit that I needed to read through the field guides later to try and absorb the subtlest of plumage details – Whiskereds are smaller, have orange-tinged eyes and are more 'coarsely' marked than Westerns.

With the distinctive song of Whip-Poor-Wills now resonating through the creek, a sound I have heard on countless Westerns but never in the raw, the time had come for our final challenge. Things were on a high. Bob spotted a tiny Common Poorwill by its eyeshine in the headlights as it absorbed the warmth of a canyon road. Everyone left the vehicle to get close up views of America's smallest nightjar, which measures little more than a Starling, and which really sings 'Poor Will Up' – the last syllable you need to be on top of the bird to hear. As we left the nightjar ruminating, it duly obliged with a three-note chorus.

Then the gremlins struck! The prerequisite for owl watching is silence. In tinder dry woodland, skirted by high rocky crags, the slightest noise is easily amplified. Each time we left the vehicle, every effort was made to dampen each footstep; talk was kept to a hushed minimum. These SAS tactics were working well and now was time to try them on the rarest of the local owl species, Flammulated.

By this stage it was pitch black and the bird was calling. Bob directed us to a strategic parking spot. We glided to a halt; vehicle doors were opened and shut in silence. Hand and head signals were working well and then... *Wow...Wow...Wow...WOW!!!* The car alarm only went off once on the entire trip – at this most inopportune moment. Every single roosting creature in Cave Creek was shaken from its slumbers. The Flammulated Owl was not just struck dumb, it more than likely took off back to its Mexican wintering grounds and remains there to this day on a diet of Prozac and Valium.

Did someone say '*Howl* Prowl?'

Cape May Revisited
New Jersey, 1999

The sea and the sky had coalesced into a seamless curtain of tempest grey that hung down from the heavens with foreboding. Clouds had been boiling for more than an hour on the eastern skyline and now, as we jogged past the million-dollar mansions of one of coastal New Jersey's most affluent neighbourhoods, gale force winds were blowing directly in our faces, sand was kicking up off the beach and the salty tang of crashing waves kissed my lips. It was late afternoon and we were heading into an imperfect storm.

Why imperfect? A little more than 16 hours into our World Series of Birding challenge and things had been going to schedule. And I mean schedule. Every minute of our attempt to see more than 200 species in a single calendar day had been worked out, refined and then ticked off on a timeline running-sheet kept in place on a clipboard cradled all day by team captain and bird race veteran Rob Unrath.

Midnight, plus one – Kearny Marsh. Check.

05.50 – High Point. Check.

14.14 – Brigantine. Check.

17.00 – Cape May. Blank.

Also on the clipboard was another printed sheet, this one carrying the WSB's soaring eagle logo and columns of North American birds which had been dutifully ticked off every time we had encountered a new species – and we had been seeing, counting and ticking them off the list at a rate of one every 5 minutes and 40 seconds.

A year on from my first outing in the grandly titled World Series I was back on the road with Rob and his friends, but this year we were gunning for the 'Big One', the whole state category in the planet's greatest birdathon. Our quest had begun in the swampy Hackensack Meadowlands that skirt the Hudson River, seen us ascending the foothills of the Appalachians, through farming communities in counties called Sussex and Middlesex and finally on the long Garden State Parkway south towards the Cape May finishing line. But, before that, we had planned to use the final few hours of daylight in the 'Capital of American Birding' to see an array of birds that would push our final tally into the 200s. As a youngster I had pored over one of John Gooders' *Where to Watch* books which had set out a monthly calendar to see 200 species in Britain in a year. Journeys to the north Norfolk coast for its migrating waders and the oak woods of Wales to hear the exotic songs of Pied Flycatchers and Wood Warblers were just two of the monthly suggestions to hit the Big Two Zero Zero. Now I hoped to achieve this feat in a mere 24 hours. It was 15.15, we still had six hours' daylight and, tallying up the crossed off boxes on our scorecard, we had just recorded our 160th bird of the day. The double ton was in sight. Most of what I had seen or heard was already a blur. There had been squealing Virginia Rails and Sora in the marshlands and a clunking Raven in the mist at High Point, the somewhat unimaginative name given to New Jersey's tallest peak, which stands at 1,803 feet. Between the Kittatinny Mountains and sea level we had seen 23 species of warbler, 20 shorebirds, 12 herons, 11 raptors, 6 thrushes and an assortment of sparrows, finches, owls and woodpeckers. I had also had the thrill of finding a much-wanted lifer, but there was no time for personal glory. This was a team sport and the team was within sight of glory. Senses were on high alert as winds howled and the skies got even darker.

You really need to be a true birder to understand the next few sentences. If you are not, you might just decide to invest in a telescope. The moment you press up close to an eyepiece and begin adjusting the focus wheel, you enter a highly magnified world of expectation and discovery. It's what makes sea watchers stare for hours on end in appalling weather. This is the raison d'etre of the raptor fanatic. One can only imagine a birder's blood pressure and pulse rate spiking as they scan the waves or the wild blue yonder and pick up the fuzzy shape of some flying creature. A few adjustments to the focus wheel, perhaps a crank of the zoom mechanism and the blur takes shape. Most times, the bird is nothing unusual, a Herring Gull in a sea of Herring Gulls. Sometimes, it vanishes before a name can be put to it – the original unidentified flying object. Sometimes, just sometimes, the hairs on your neck begin rise and your mouth begins to dry as some distant sprite takes shape and you can make your call. 'Greater Shearwater!' I screamed at the top of my voice. 'Greater Shearwater,' I repeated for good measure. 'About 400 yards out but it keeps disappearing below the swell!'

My teammates gathered round wanting a piece of the action through my scope. I had found the bird of the day, perhaps the bird of the entire competition, a 'write in' species, one that the organisers deem too rare to be named on the official printed scorecard competitors hand in at the end of the race. Each one of the team took turns to look out over the crashing sea and gave the thumbs up once they had seen the shearwater careening from side to side on starch stiff wings, toying with the waves being thrown up by the twisting anger of low rain clouds. Not that choppy waters trouble such a masterful mariner as the Greater Shearwater, the original rider of the storm.

Greater Shearwaters perform one of the most remarkable migrations of any bird. After leaving their breeding grounds on Tristan da Cunha and a few other rocky outcrops in the South Atlantic during the northern hemisphere's winter, they undertake a ten-month clockwise sweep around the Atlantic, passing Brazil and America's Eastern Seaboard before heading east to British waters and then the final leg, the long flight across the Equator and back to their nesting burrows. If the weather conditions are right in spring, a few turn up along the US coastline. Today I was lucky. Or was I? The weather patterns that had carried the shearwater into focus were now brewing a storm to end all storms.

We were no more than 15 miles from Cape May's famous lighthouse and the finishing line. Along the way, there were dozens of potential new birds to see in and around the mighty Delaware Estuary, species at the most northerly extremes of their range. Here, we would add Carolina Chickadee to the Black-capped species we had seen in the New Jersey hills. Yellow-throated Warbler, arguably the most beautiful *Dendroica*, occurred in Cape May County in small numbers. The same went for Blue Grosbeak and White-eyed Vireo. There was a chance of American Avocet and we would certainly see Black Skimmers *if* things went well.

It was to prove a big if. My 'Strictly for the Birds' column, published on 17 May 1996, takes up the story:

The American dream vanished the moment the thick, black clouds crept over the horizon and took on an ominous shape. We had driven twice the distance of a Formula One grand prix and had been on our feet for 15 back-breaking hours. Birds had come and gone as our jeep had crawled up mountains, splashed through swamps and raced along sandy beach tracks. Our tally in the World Series of Birding stood at a respectable 160 species and we had not reached the city limits of Cape May – America's finest location for finding birds.

Then we saw the clouds. Not ordinary clouds but a twisting, swirling mass of black fury. I had come to America to witness bird migration in all its glory and, instead, faced nature's most awesome phenomenon: a tornado.

As the twister danced over the New Jersey coastline all hopes of us getting the magic 200 bird sightings we needed for a decent placing in the WSB ended. The storm chucked down two inches of rain over the next six hours, the same six hours we had hoped would give us the host of missing birds on our checklist.

When the final scores were revealed the next morning it was obvious that wiser contestants had used the weather conditions to their advantage. The winning team, from America's *Birder's World* magazine, had recorded a record-breaking 229 species – 66 more than our final figure.

On paper, our team had all the pedigree to get a good total. Captain Rob Unrath has the best ears for bird sounds I've ever encountered, while the other two members were both well-travelled and respected American birders, yet for all our efforts and weeks of careful planning, we finished 21st out of 44 teams. Only when I drew my first relaxed breath after all our exertions did it dawn that I had just experienced the best day's birding of my life. Where could I hope to see 163 different species in a day in Europe? When did I last see 23 species of warbler in 24 hours?

And had I not just seen the most eagerly sought tick on my US list? The Yellow-throated Vireo, a bird that has long mesmerised British twitchers, and eluded me since it first turned up in Cornwall in September 1990, was just one of the highlights of my day.

Our 510-mile route around New Jersey, from the shoreline opposite Manhattan to Atlantic City, created enough memories for a lifetime. And not only was it pure pleasure. The efforts of all the teams raised £300,000 for conservation.

I'm already planning next year's challenge...

As it turned out, the twister that took shape over the Jersey Shore put paid to my bird-racing days on the other side of the Atlantic. In 1997 I was a member of a Bedfordshire team that won the inland category of *Birdwatch* magazine's annual bird race completion and, in 2004, I participated in Finland's crazy 24-hour Kuusamo competition which takes place under the midnight sun and messes up the body clock for weeks. Whether it was the experience of seeing our challenge literally blown away by natural forces, or the realisation that there are only so many spring migrations in a birder's lifetime and there is a big world to explore, the thrills and adrenalin buzz of seeing a score of warblers before a breakfast of Snickers Bars and Gatorade are a happy, but distant, memory. Nevertheless, the lure of Cape May and the unpredictability of its weather conditions are a hard addiction to give up. I knew I would return one day.

Three years later, in September 1999, I was on a tour bus heading south along a minor coastal road towards the Cape May resort. The wipers were struggling to keep up with a deluge that had turned the windscreen into a bubbling cascade. A weatherman came on the radio. His voice was stern.

'Hurricane Floyd is expected to hit Cape May around 1 p.m.,' he warned.

With a look at my watch and the vehicle's speedometer and then a quick calculation, I worked out that 1 p.m. was our ETA, too. The biggest, most destructive storm to hit America's eastern states for years just happened to coincide with the autumn tour I was co-leading to New Jersey for its wader, warbler and raptor migration.

Upon arrival on a warm September evening, I had announced to the group, somewhat naively, that the impending cyclone might 'blow some good birds in'. Two days later I was praying that the 80 mph gusts would not simply blow us away. We were in good hands. The driver was a tough ex-marine who had spent most of his adult life carrying out conservation surveys in America's wildest regions. Nothing fazed him. He had the calmness of a veteran who had survived the horrors of the Korean War and all manner of nature's most powerful, destructive forces. He held the steering wheel firmly and pressed ahead. Outside, road signs were clattering, power lines twanged and the winds howled, but our tour bus proceeded slowly and surely. Wind and rain would not stop us arriving in Cape May.

The journey took us past the spot where the tornado had formed and destroyed my WSB dreams three years before, and through the resort's sedate neighbourhoods with their ornate and colourful houses that dated back to an age when American presidents came to the lower Jersey Shore for their summer retreat. Along the beach road, late-season tourists were battling against the wind in cagoules that flapped like parachutes, their hands held over their faces to protect them from the eroding blasts of rainwater mixed with beach sand and salty sea spray. A row of TV vans was parked up along the sea front, satellite dishes at the ready to broadcast the story of America's most powerful hurricane of the season.

Floyd was named in the tradition of choosing alternate male and female names alphabetically as the hurricane season progressed. It seemed a good choice. Someone in the van said the storm had a knockout blow like the great, two-times world heavyweight champion Floyd Patterson. As I opened the front passenger door to get out, I was almost knocked off my feet by the force of the wind and rain. Along the street, TV reporters were trying to give live bulletins in their immaculate power suits and make-up while holding on to umbrellas (and that was just the guys).

Off shore, the birds seemed oblivious to the winds. Sandwich Terns were flying low over water, pointed wings expertly adjusting their posture at every gust. The Laughing Gulls appeared to be laughing in the face of the wind and sheet rain. Our group huddled under a storm shelter at the end of the beach road and watched the spectacular unfold. Tiny Sanderlings that had recently taken on their white winter garb looked like snowballs as they were sent tumbling along the beach. Most of the other shorebirds had departed to Cape May's freshwater marshes but the resident flock of Black Skimmer had hunkered down in the sand, their preposterous lower-mandibles dug in deep and acting as anchors.

For more than an hour the rains raged, the winds blew and we marvelled at the ability of birds to fly in such horrendous conditions. Then, the winds began to ease as if they were at the mercy of a control switch. Rains that could have taken skin off moments before calmed to a fine, misty spray. The dark battleship-grey sky lightened to the pearly tones of the mantle of the Ring-billed Gull which was now nonchalantly scouring the streets for tasty flotsam. Hurricane Floyd's eye was looking down at us, inspecting his handiwork. Shutters came off buildings. The television folk went live once more. I went birding.

Somehow, I had expected to witness a marvellous fall of migrating songbirds and for the magnolias and myrtle trees that brought spring colours to Cape May to be full of Magnolia and Myrtle Warblers. Perhaps that most elusive and diffident of all American passerines, the skulking Connecticut Warbler, would cut short its journey and hunker until Floyd bade farewell. The skies, I convinced myself, should also be beating to the wings of raptors held up over the Delaware Estuary. Storms back home in

Bedfordshire always seemed to deliver windfalls. Why not in the home of American birding? Weather bulletins, and later rationalising, explained why there were no southbound migrants to be seen. Hurricane Floyd was the third major hurricane of the 1999 season and triggered the third largest evacuation in US history as 2.6 million people living along the coast across five states were ordered from their homes. Floyd had been germinated in the warm, moist Atlantic waters off Cape Verde before heading westwards and striking the Bahamas and then finally hurtling due north. During the hurricane's 12-day lifetime it almost reached Category 5, the highest rating on the Saffir-Simpson Scale, with sustained winds of around 150 mph. What set Floyd apart was its menacing track along the Atlantic States, depositing huge amounts of rainfall on the highly populated narrow ribbon of coastal settlements. Chestertown in Maryland reported up to 14 inches of rain in as many hours and floods that would last weeks. Tragically, 57 people lost their lives, six of them in New Jersey. Experts spoke of it as a 'once-in-a-few-centuries' event and the total clean-up bill was in the billions.

As I walked around in the strange, humid conditions of the storm's eye, with its eerie silence – there was no birdsong – it dawned; any storm-blown birds that arrived at Cape May would obviously have a southern provenance. I racked my brain but, with my limited understanding of North American bird movements, it seemed unlikely that in autumn there would be northerly overshoots, while the migratory birds due to head against the northerly track of the storm knew instinctively what to do: stay put. With the skies darkening once more, the winds beginning to pick up and heavy drops of rain starting to fall, I hurried back to the hotel. Hurricane Floyd part II – the reverse side of the eye – was about to strike.

The rains continued overnight and into the next day. Next morning, the news bulletins were dominated by horrific images and tragic stories. Children were among the drowning victims. Outside, Cape May appeared to have escaped lightly. Scattered branches, windblown jetsam and bits of flapping roof were about as bad as it got. There even seemed to be bird movement overhead. Sharp-shinned and Cooper's Hawks were powering through low over the rooftops. A Merlin dashed by in pursuit of a terrified Tree Swallow. The orange glow of Monarch butterfly wings added a dash of seasonal colour. Scores of these beautifully patterned but toxic insects were fluttering in the sky. A young Merlin grabbed at one and hurriedly spat it out; the poisonous chemicals the butterflies had absorbed from eating milkweed would not save this individual but the falcon had learned to leave them alone in the future.

Cape May's famous hawk platform seemed the best place for the tour group to spend the remainder of the day. Survey workers were busy turning dots high in the sky into raptor statistics on a scorecard. Headlining the list of Peregrines, Merlins, Northern Harriers, Red-tailed, Sharp-shinned and Cooper's Hawks were four Bald Eagles. I nodded to show I was impressed.

'You should have been here yesterday.' The Cape May veteran spoke as if he was disappointed with his raptor tally.

'We were,' I responded, explaining that we had arrived during the height of Hurricane Floyd.

'We spent an hour or so sea watching and picked up a few Sandwich Terns battling in the winds. That was a new American bird for me,' I added for effect.

The veteran seemed even less impressed. He asked where we had spent the storm and I signalled the storm-shelter a mile or so up the coast.

'You should have been over there,' he said nodding beyond the lighthouse towards Cape May Point and the mouth of the Delaware.

'The locals had more than 40 Sooty Terns, 10 Bridled Terns, 30 Parasitic Jaegers, a Wilson's Storm-Petrel and many phalaropes,' he spoke as if he was reciting the prizes on a game show. 'It was one of the best days birding in Cape May's history. Some are saying it was the best.' I went into a trance. Even I knew that Sooty and Bridled Terns were highly prized tropical birds, mega rarities on both sides of the Atlantic. As Hurricane Floyd had hit the Bahamas they must have flown north, perhaps taking sanctuary safe in the cyclone's eye where flying conditions would have been a lot more comfortable. One could only guess where the terns had ended up.

The tour group looked crestfallen when I told them that we had missed such rarities by being in the wrong place. I expected a lynching, but one of the participants smiled and said: 'There's always tomorrow.'

To prove that very point, long before dawn the next morning we were clambering up a muddy bank overlooking Cape May's Higbee Beach in anticipation of an event that has become my number one birding spectacle. American wood-warblers are my favourite group of birds. Seeing these gaudy sprites decorating a tree with their brilliant rainbow colours never fails to lift the heart and embolden the spirit. Every birdwatcher should make a pilgrimage to America to witness their grace and beauty. For most birders this would mean a spring visit, when the males are at their dazzling best and drawing attention with their high-pitched songs.

True wood-warbler aficionados, however, cannot wait until autumn, when songs are replaced by a confounding repertoire of chip notes and fresh, dowdy plumages are still months from morphing into the brilliant costumes of spring. With populations bolstered several hundred per cent by newly fledged young in their confusing autumn uniforms, the thrill of solving the identification mysteries more than makes up for the reduction in any colour quality. Autumn also delivers a much better chance of seeing migrating birds in concentrated numbers, and if any place in

America proves this point, then it is the muddy 12-foot bank known affectionately as Higbee Dike.

The diehards were already in situ, taking their positions on the muddy mound as if they were laying claim to their favourite positions on a football terrace. Silence prevailed. Acquaintances smiled at old friends. Whispered hellos greeted new faces. Dawn's early light illuminated the eastern skyline. A Solitary Sandpiper heralded the new day with its shrill alarm notes. And then it began.

A dark shape zipped in front of my face. Another followed. Black scintillas sparkled and flashed around us. Squeaky calls, most too similar for me to differentiate, grew in volume. More black shapes appeared from nowhere. The quietness that had been maintained among the 100-strong crowd vanished. Bird names were shouted out as if people were reading through checklists. 'Bay-breasted... Blackburnian... Blackpoll...'

There was almost an alphabetic order to the names being called out, but there was nothing orderly about what was happening before our eyes. The birds were in a flying frenzy, darting and dashing in all directions. For an instant, I was reminded of a disturbed flock of Meadow Pipits, as each bird's silhouette seemed identical in the half-light. For the Higbee Dike diehards, the chaos and the poor light conditions only added to the excitement of deducing an identity from limited clues.

'Black-throated Blue... Black-throated Green... Cape May...'

The commentary became as frenetic as what could only be described as an avian pyrotechnics show continued all around. Birds were whizzing past at head height. Binoculars were all but useless at such close quarters. The experts relied on their ears and an innate knowledge of wood-warbler jizz, assessing tail-length and wing shape, bulk and flight pattern with the speed of a supercomputer. I had long held my hands up in surrender. Years of learning spring and autumn plumages, endless hours of listening to birdsong, had not prepared me for such a challenge. Only when the light had improved so that it was possible to pick the patterns and colours of the commoner species was I confident of calling out individual birds.

'Parula... Wilson's... Yellow-rumped...'

Putting the group on to individual birds was as difficult as making firm identities. The swirling mass made it impossible to keep track of a marked out bird. Higbee veterans had been calling out names constantly but connecting them to the silhouettes flying around our heads was impossible. I thought I heard someone call out 'Connecticut' in the migrant melee, but even though a bulkier, seemingly longer-winged warbler shot by, I just had to accept defeat and a building realisation that I would never see a bird that I had now renamed 'Confounding Warbler'.

Then it was over. The oohs and aahs of the excited Higbee Dikers faded. Expert commentaries stopped. A cloud of birds as dynamic and energetic as the tornado I had witnessed three years before evaporated. For less than an hour, I had been engulfed in a migration spectacular like no other. Any recriminating thoughts I had about my ability to put names to the ethereal shapes were healed by a friendly American in a checked shirt and baseball cap.

'That was tough!' he admitted. 'Those warblers sure play games. I've been coming every day for the past few weeks and still cannot get a handle on most, er, hardly any of them.' I agreed.

'You're a Brit!' The middle-aged American exclaimed, seemingly baffled as to why any British birder would be masochistic enough to suffer the Higbee Dike experience. He pondered, adjusting his cap bedecked with bird badges from all over the world.

'Do your warblers in England behave the same way?' he asked.

I nodded disconsolately. He smiled.

'I guess you're relieved about that with all those, what d'ya call them, er, li'l brown jobs? I have read about the chiff-er-what and the Willow Warbler. Sounds real tough...'

I agreed but said it was a lot easier studying a Chiffchaff when it was perched. Identifying one in flight, especially among a flock of other warblers, would be a challenge for the best of birders. In all my years, I had never seen anything like the explosion of migrant passerines we had just witnessed, but why had all those American wood-warblers behaved in such a way?

'Sure beats me,' he admitted. 'There were a lot more birds this morning than previous days. Hurricane Floyd was most probably the reason for that, but why we get these clouds of warblers like Monarch butterflies most days of autumn? You'll have to ask a better birder than me...'

For the rest of the morning that was the question on my lips, but I never did get a satisfactory answer until several years later, and the causes of the Higbee experience remain 'proposed explanations' rather than cast iron reasons.

One suggestion is 'forced migration': nocturnal migrants are compelled to continue flying during the day because they are over unsuitable habitat such as open water where landing is impossible. Another is 're-determined migration', which is most often witnessed in coastal areas and possibly occurs because birds have drifted away from primary migration routes because of prevailing winds. Then there is 'onward migration', when nocturnal passerine migrants take a lead from waders and wildfowl and continue flying long into the day to make better progress. And the final theory is 'resumed migration': after taking a rest during the night, nocturnal migrants resume their flights during the early daylight hours.

Still in awe of what we had witnessed, the group left the dike and wandered through the woods and fields that make the Higbee Beach Wildlife Management Area probably the most watched birding site on the planet. There were scores, perhaps hundreds, of people scouring the scrub, grassland and wooded glades for migrants. Groups gathered where the birds congregated. Mixed flocks of warblers worked the sprigs and snags for insects; birders worked below them for good views and positive IDs. Thankfully, migrant Rose-breasted Grosbeaks, Baltimore Orioles, Scarlet Tanagers and Yellow-billed Cuckoos were loafing in the leaf canopy after their arduous journeys, allowing brilliant scope views of marvellous shades of pinks and yellows. The trees also held a full hand of vireos – Red-eyed, Warbling, Philadelphia, Blue-headed and White-eyed – and these were only slightly more energetic as they moved through the branches in their normal, cautious manner. Northern Flickers, in numbers you would never expect for a woodpecker, made rippling flights hither and thither, performing hurried landings whenever the shape of a raptor cast a shadow. And there were plenty of marauding falcons and accipiters about to strike at the unwary.

There was one warbler that even the sharpest-eyed Merlin or the most resolute hawk would struggle to vanquish. For all the showiness of *Dendroica*, the delicate colours of *Vermivora* and the frenetic behaviour of *Wilsonia*, one genus seemed to have been put on Earth to confound birders: the diffident, skulking *Oporornis*, whose name derives from the Greek for 'autumn birds'. Kentucky, Mourning and Connecticut Warblers are difficult enough to find in spring when they are on territory and in full song. In autumn they take on the mantles of Western Palearctic Locustellas, working the ground like furtive rodents. Arguably, the chunky Connecticut Warbler, with its yellowish plumage, white spectacles and flesh-pink legs is the most difficult passerine to track down in North America. Its deep Atlantic migration route, as well as a long wing projection, makes the Connecticut a prime candidate for vagrancy in the UK, but an ability to melt away in straw-coloured autumn vegetation means it has yet to be found in Europe. Of all the North American warblers, this was the one I wanted to see most.

The very name Connecticut, which derives from the Native American word *Quinnehtukqut* meaning 'beside the long tidal river', had fascinated me as a youngster, especially after seeing Bing Crosby's black-and-white classic, *A Connecticut Yankee in King Arthur's Court*. Listening to Americans speaking about them in the same way as British birders talk about 'Lancies' (Lanceolated Warbler) and 'PG Tips' (Pallas's Grasshopper Warbler), only added to their mystique.

As we walked Higbee's grassy trails, stopping to absorb the sunray brightness of a glorious Yellow-breasted Chat and watch Black-throated Blue Warblers gorge on berries à la Blackcap, a flash of olive-yellow caught my eye. A head poked out and I am sure a beady eye with a white ring clocked me and then disappeared back into the grass.

I wanted to shout out the line I had been planning since the first hour we had arrived in Cape May – 'I've just connected with a Connecticut!' – but the blighter had upstaged me by performing to type. Checking a field guide later, my eyes were drawn to its scientific name, *Oporornis agilis*. It did not take a Classics don to work out what it meant – the 'elusive, agile bird of autumn'.

Stung into Action
Panama, 2005

The peace of a new day is shattered by the sound of the neighbours moving a piano across a newly polished floor. The screeching and scraping lasts an age, rudely interrupting a wonderful dream and seriously testing my patience at a time when the sun has yet to appear on the horizon. Then it dawns: there are no people living upstairs. I'm 80 feet up in the rainforest canopy. Curiosity kicks in. What could have disturbed the stillness? I open the shutters and, out of the gloom, the unmistakable shape of a long-limbed monkey comes crashing through the spindly branches of a giant cecropia tree and stares me full in the face. I forget all the advised protocols about making eye-to-eye contact with a large primate and look back, angrily. I am tired and jet-lagged. The monkey shows his displeasure by letting loose the most amazing, blood-curdling scream imaginable.

By the time he screams again, my room-mate, the celebrated wildlife photographer David Tipling, is at work, firing off portrait shots of our guest as he screeches and wails to his heart's content.

David captures the primate in all its magnificence: powerful limbs and a thick, woolly coat of chocolate brown worn like a monk's cowl, framing an endearing face. The monkey's morning prayer call rips through the forest once more. It's easy to understand why this particular primate was named the Mantled Howler Monkey.

Howlers provide the unrequested but appreciated early alarm calls at Panama's famous Canopy Tower eco-tourism retreat. A dawn start is vital if you wish to catch the forest 'rush hour' in all its glory. Creatures are waking to a new day, breaking the 12-hour fast imposed by the inky tropical night. The tree tops are alive with the flickering and bickering of birds breakfasting and conducting their morning ablutions. This was once a secret world, far out of reach of human interference, but we now have a window into the daily soap opera of rainforest life, courtesy of Uncle Sam. Canopy Tower is the reincarnation of a United States Air Force listening post built deep in the lowland rainforest to safeguard the Panama Canal at a time when the Cold War was at its chilliest. For purists, the sight of a 100 foot tall metal construction with a huge fibre glass 'golf ball' – which once housed top secret surveillance equipment – is an abomination in the pristine forest, but today the tower is a monument to sustainable tourism and conservation. Thirty years after it was picking up the shadows of oil tankers and tourist ships and detecting the movement of light aircraft laden with narcotics, the tower was sold off. Fortunately, one of Panama's most distinguished figures, former politician, businessmen and committed environmentalist Raul Arias de Para took it under his wing.

Raul, grandson of Don Tomás Arias, one of the founders of the Republic of Panama, served two terms in the national assembly and was twice held prisoner by the despotic and corrupt General Manuel Noriega before emerging after his country's liberation as a major figure in its reconstruction as a democracy. In 1994, driven by a dream of saving a waterfall close to his heart, he entered the world of eco-tourism and three years later signed a long-term contract with his government to transform the decrepit, corrugated metal monstrosity into the marvel it is today.

Climbing on to the tower's 360-degree observation deck that first morning, I let out a 'wow' almost as loud as the cry of the howler monkey. Nothing had prepared me for the view that stretched out to the glistening Pacific and the skyscrapers of Panama City far in the distance. Between my forest vantage point and the hustle and bustle of one of Central America's busiest metropolises stretched a forest adorned in the ethereal shroud of morning mist. The tallest trees poked out of this white fluffiness like pepper pots set on a table cloth of pure linen and the silhouettes of early-rising parrots shot across the vista as if they were crumbs. David, his memory card already bursting with howler monkey portraits, put his landscape lens to work. My mind's eye was also capturing the moment at 1/10,000th of a second at F1. Nothing had prepared me for the Panamanian panorama when I arrived at Canopy Tower in the dark the previous evening with David and two of the birding world's best known writers, Mark Cocker and Jonathan Elphick. We were at the start of an adventure that would excite, entertain and ultimately leave its mark on me in many ways. Mark's beautiful crafting of the English language has done so much to educate and enlighten on the subject of birds, but even his observational skills and wide vocabulary seemed unable to define what unfolded before us as the morning haze melted away to reveal a forest of countless greens. They say a Woodpigeon's eye has the capacity to detect 10,000 separate shades of green but even the most accomplished retina would have struggled to accommodate such a verdant overload. Fortunately, amid the greens, other colours began to radiate.

All colours of the rainbow were represented in the birds that went about their business oblivious to the binoculars and telescopes at work on our forest lookout. Red-lored Amazons, one of Panama's largest parrots, darted about in pairs like loved-up couples incapable of independent thought. Smaller, cuter, Orange-chinned Parakeets squawked their way to and fro in garrulous flocks, highly visible whenever their leaf-coloured plumages were backlit by clear sky. We continued working through the spectrum. Yellow-crowned Euphonias, finch-like birds with colour schemes that would confound even the most avant-garde interior designer – a combination of deep purple and free-range yolk yellow – played tag among the uppermost branches. They were one of three species of euphonia – the name derives from its 'excellence of tone' – that we watched with fascination although we never heard them calling.

By now, we were reaching the middle frequencies of our journey through the electromagnetic spectrum. Parrots and parakeets had already given us our daily greens but two other species with the colour in their name were both present, the smart, jade-toned Green Honeycreeper and the noisy Green Shrike-vireo, whose three-syllable 'look up here' song provided the mood music of every subsequent visit to the top deck. With Blue Dacnis, a small turquoise tanager, and Violet-bellied Hummingbird, we had all but finished our quest to find the colours of the rainbow in the forest canopy. But where were we going to find anything indigo? One of the guides then pointed far below to the forest floor where Indigo Buntings, long-distance travellers from the US, spent the winter foraging for seeds. We looked intently for these small, brilliantly coloured birds but sadly never found what would have been our avian pot of gold at the end of the rainbow.

Throughout our forest vigil, the cornflower-blue skies had billowed with the shapes of thousands of Turkey Vultures commuting towards the distant cityscape, their incredible olfactory senses on alert for anything in a state of decay. Some American vultures, whose accepted evolutionary perch has shifted between storks and true raptors and may now deserve a branch all of its own, can pick up traces of ethyl mercaptan, a chemical given off by rotting flesh, from great distances. Once Turkey Vultures have picked up a scent, the closely related Black Vulture and also the impressive King Vulture, neither having an advanced sense of smell, latch on to the 'TVs' and follow them to the rotting carrion, bullying them on the ground into giving up their meal.

Canopy Tower is one of the great places on the planet to witness raptor migration and some days the skies are blackened with swirling kettles of migrating Broad-winged Hawks which, together with the vultures, produce counts in excess of 100,000 birds.

The howler monkey reveille followed by the climb to the observation deck became the routine over the following mornings although it was far from being a *Groundhog Day* experience. Every morning the trees were decked with different shapes and colours as cotingas, tanagers and puzzling flycatchers vied for our attention. An outrageous Keel-billed Toucan was the odds-on favourite to win the prize for our most preposterous sighting until someone spotted the funnels of a giant passenger cruiser chugging in a straight line through the heart of the forest. It was easy to forget Canopy Tower's origins as radar cover for the Panama Canal and its shipping.

History lessons about this fascinating country at the thinnest point of the Central American isthmus became a constant feature of days out in the field with the tower's team of guides. A tutorial about General Noriega's brutal regime and his eventual downfall following the US invasion of 1989 was made all the more intriguing when we visited the boarded up villa-cum-bunker where he used to relax before he was sentenced to spend the next 30 years in a rather less spacious North American prison cell. At the height of Noriega's drug-financed rule, the despot's lair would have been guarded by the cream of his presidential guard but, on the day we visited, only two rusty-toned Aplomado Falcons were standing sentinel on a tree overlooking his hideout.

Cynics may think that American influences cut through Panamanian life as deeply and influentially as the 48-mile canal that joins the Pacific to the Caribbean. Yes, you can pay a bar bill with Yankee greenbacks or watch beautiful young women in the latest Rodeo Drive designer labels driving imported sports utility vehicles. Indeed, Panamanians joke that the McDonald's franchises and skyscrapers have turned their capital into the 'Miami of the South'. Snowbirds – American tourists looking to escape the winter frosts of New England – migrate each autumn to soak up the rays on idyllic sandy beaches; American birders hooked on the avian wonders of the Neotropics make similar journeys without having to punish their credit cards or travel inordinate distances across South America to build their bird lists. And what a list Panama boasts! Although only the size of Scotland, it has a national list of 950 species, 105 of which are regional endemics and 12 full endemics. Little wonder, therefore, that the visitors' book of Canopy Tower reads like a *Who's Who* of the American birding scene. Among the noted dignitaries who have stayed there are tour leader Victor Emmanuel, artist David Sibley and Jimmy Carter, 39th President of the United States and confirmed birder. Although American influences run deep throughout Panama, it is the power of the rainforest to entwine, envelope and finally obliterate all signs of mankind that was to leave me with my most poignant – and painful – memories of the country.

The Pipeline Road is arguably the best place to birdwatch on Earth. More birds have been seen along this stretch of overgrown dirt track in a single day than anywhere else on the planet. In 1985, the Panama Audubon Society's Christmas Bird Count clocked up a Guinness World Record with an astonishing 385 species in 24 hours. Only four decades earlier, Pipeline Road stood between the US and disaster after it was carved through impenetrable forest to become a vital fuel line in the event of the Japanese attacking the Panama Canal. The invasion never came. The US, with a great deal of help from the British Empire, won the war of the Pacific and the Pipeline Road was slowly swallowed up by nature.

Tantalising promises of a day's birding on Pipeline Road had been our guides' way of driving us from dawn to dusk – and well beyond – during our stay at Canopy Tower. Not that we needed much encouragement to clamber to the observation deck before sunrise, march through mangrove swamps and dry scrub during the heat of the day and then go on nocturnal, spotlight safaris deep in the forest when the sloths were not so slothful and Greater Bulldog Fishing Bats went to work, snatching tiddlers from murky ponds with their sharp claws.

Hoffman's Two-toed Sloths are particularly endearing creatures. By day, they hang around – literally – in tall trees looking like bundles of old clothes put out to dry. Not that their fur has ever been near a washing machine. Indeed, a sloth's pelt is so rank that it develops an ecosystem of its own, with the mangy-looking, algae-covered fur providing sanctuary for moths and flying insects. Brown-throated Three-toed Sloths with distinctive bandit-style face markings are also found in the forest, but their fur always looked as if their coats had been well cleansed by a proprietary detergent. The ever-noisy howler monkeys and the delightful Geoffroy's Tamarind, a small red-headed monkey, meant that the primates were well and truly represented, and a cute Kinkajou made a fascinating spotlight find as it did its best to impersonate Gollum, the freakish creature of *Lord of the Rings* fame, staring down with eyes the size of saucers. My favourite forest creature, however, was the bizarre but endearing Northern Tamandua, an arboreal anteater with the supine ease of a sloth and a snout to die for.

These forest creatures do not give up their whereabouts easily. Dense foliage and camouflage markings keep them well obscured from prying eyes, but we had a secret weapon, one of Canopy Tower's brilliant and personable guides, Carlos Bethancourt.

Carlos, a young Panamanian, used his forest guile and deep knowledge of its creatures to keep us continually awestruck with an endless supply of wildlife experiences. Whether it was showing us recently fledged Spectacled Owls making a spectacle as they gave us the quizzical eye, picking out the soft, chicken-like call of a Slaty-tailed Trogon amid the cacophony of birdsong or finding brilliantly coloured poison dart frogs, Carlos had a knack of always having a ready anecdote to add piquancy to his discoveries.

One morning, our conversation got round to the forest's serpents and I told Carlos about an incident a friend in the military had witnessed in Belize involving the fearsome Fer-de-lance, a pit viper with a reputation for being easily agitated. The snake had been so riled that it had actually attacked an army vehicle as it drove past and had punctured the metal body work with a row of fang bites.

Carlos rolled up his trousers to reveal a fist-sized scar on his calf caused by this highly venomous snake. The incredibly painful bite had almost proved fatal and iresulted in a long stay in hospital suffering from the effects of haemotoxin, a venom which destroys the body's red blood cells, disrupts blood clotting and causes organ degeneration. But he had another story.

'I was bitten by a Bullet Ant when I was a child and it felt more painful than being bitten by the Fer-de-Lance,' Carlos explained as we headed along the Pipeline Road for a new day's birding. He went on to explain how the ant was once used in initiation ceremonies for young tribesman and that the ant's name had been given by the first Spanish Conquistadors who thought they had been shot by musket balls, such was the pain inflicted by a single sting. Looking at Carlos's scar and listening to the story of his near-death experience had put me on DEFCON 1 as far as snakes were concerned, but an ant sting? That was nothing, I told myself as I recollected the day I had to have a bee sting removed from a particularly sensitive part of my anatomy when I was still in short trousers. Anyway, it was antbirds rather than ants that were supposed to be occupying our minds.

If wood-warblers are the star turn in North America, then it is the antbird family that holds pride of place for producing the most thrills in the tropics. Admittedly, antbirds are not as colourful as the tanagers or as charismatic as the cotingas. They do not create conservation concerns like the macaws or have the majesty of Harpy Eagles or Andean Condors. What antbirds do provide is action, the thrill of the hunt and a masterclass in Darwin's teachings on natural selection. Every biology student knows the story of Charles Darwin and his observations of Galapagos Finches, which led him to propose that the birds had adapted to different habitats and food sources across the archipelago. Hence, at the extreme ends of this 16-strong group, we see the delicate Warbler Finch with its fine bill for feeding on insects and then, at the other extreme, the bruising Vegetarian Finch and its beak of grosbeak-like proportions. If Darwin had taken his research deep into the forests of South America he would have been totally consumed by the multiplicity of the antbirds and may never have finished his seminal *On the Origin of Species*. There are, in fact, more than 200 species in the family Thamnophilidae and all are named according to other passerines they resemble. Antshrikes, antvireos and antwrens fill the ranks of the less imaginatively described antbirds. Closely related families, the Formicariidae and Grallariidae, bolster the list with ground-loving antthrushes and antpittas.

During our excursions into the forest, Carlos had already picked out a number of antbirds going about their business, exploiting their niches as nature intended. He expertly imitated the call of a Streak-chested Antpitta, a bird that looked like someone had taken a tennis ball, splattered it with ink spots and then stuck on two incongruously long-legs, and also found a beautifully marked Ocellated Antbird for David to capture on film in all its coppery-toned glory. Such intimate encounters only increased the currency of these fascinating and elusive beauties. Fleeting glimpses and a few close encounters of singletons going about their daily toils – a crake-like Black-faced Antthrush was particularly good at playing hide-and-seek on the edges of a swamp – had left us longing to see the forest's main event: an antbird feeding frenzy. For this you need army ants, thousands of them. When these guys go on manoeuvres the forest quakes. Determined battalions of insects cut through the forest floor as if they are road-building. Their scurrying labours clear metre-wide ant highways, piling leaf-litter either side to form what look like crash barriers. Anything that moves in the fast lane is run down, stung and consumed. Those creatures that escape the tumultuous horde are ripe for picking-off by the army's 'camp followers', the ant birds.

I cannot honestly remember if it was Carlos's acute hearing that picked out one of the antbird's calls to muster or if his sharp eyes detected the ripples of a million heaving insect bodies, but after days of scouring the forest it was happening. The ants had left the safety of their bivouacs and were on the hunt. Scouting parties had left chemical signals for their brothers-in-arms – strictly speaking, sisters – and now the invasion force was cutting a trail alongside the Pipeline Road humans had made more than 60 years earlier. As spiders, beetles, scorpions, millipedes, grasshoppers and countless other creepies began frantically crawling away on all manner of spindly legs, the antbirds arrived in force to pick off the invertebrate diaspora. The show had begun.

Above the mass of ants, tiny birds were darting and flicking in all directions, resting on sprigs to work out their strategy to plunder the ants' potential prey without becoming consumed themselves. Three or four stings would easily be enough to kill a small passerine. A striking Barred Antshrike reminded me of a flying barcode as it zipped down to seize an unfortunate bug. A Bicoloured Antbird with its big, turquoise orbital ring set in a face of warm chestnut hung like a circus artist on the thinnest of vines waiting for its moment to strike. Close by, a Spotted Antbird declared itself ready for action, puffing out a snow-white breast liberally decorated with a necklace of black teardrop markings. The so-called 'Three Amigos' were also busy at work. The amigos are species of antwren that have formed a forest triumvirate in a strategy that biologists call 'microniche portioning' – the bird world's equivalent of football positions. Dot-winged Antwrens scour the densest vines, White-flanked Antwrens head for more open areas and Checker-throated Antwrens prefer dead foliage. Competition is thus dramatically reduced and each species gets a fair share of the plunder. Swarms are such a part of forest feeding behaviour that other birds also take advantage of the invertebrate food on offer. Woodcreepers are particularly adept at winkling out insects from crinkly sections of bark with their large curved bills, behaviour reminiscent of treecreepers in other continents and another great example of convergent evolution at work.

The endless procession of tiny bodies cascading across the forest floor continued to cause consternation among ground-dwelling creatures and draw in more birds. A Rufous Motmot, a New World equivalent of a bee-eater, which inhabits forest and teams a sickly mustard-coloured chest with emerald green wings, could just about be made out high in the canopy. Smaller woodland sprites were less easy to identify. How many tanagers and migratory wood-warblers were present, one can only guess. Each tree seemed to harbour a bird, yet as the spectacle continued, our desire for better views and closer encounters began to draw us into the forest and away from the sanctuary of the Pipeline Road.

I must have only taken ten steps off-road when I noticed a large ant climbing on Jonathan's shoulders and nonchalantly went to flick it away. Most insects would simply have rolled with the blow from a finger well versed in the art of Subbuteo. Instead, the devil clung to my nail for dear life – and then exacted wicked revenge.

Think of your most painful experience and double it. No, treble it. Quadruple it. Think of your finger first being set on fire, then ceremoniously slammed in a car door and, after that, forced into the swirling blades of a food-blender before finally having acid poured into the wound.

I screamed like a banshee before running back towards the road with the ant still in situ, no doubt enjoying every second of my misery. I remember little else. The pain kept surging up my arm and into my chest, taking my breath away. Mark, David, Jonathan and Carlos looked on speechless as I performed a demented tarantella, holding my finger and watching it throb in the style of a Tom and Jerry cartoon. I have faint recollections of David dropping his trousers to remove an ant from his nether regions while Jonathan stoically suffered a bite without a murmur. I cried.

The pain lasted three hours, 180 minutes of agony made all the worse by the enduring topic of conversation – Bullet Ant stings. Carlos's soothing words about the ant's reputation did little for the pain but made me feel less of a wimp. The others conducted an inquest into the incident, recalling second by second what had happened up to my abject screaming out as if I had been targeted by a sniper. Only when I returned home did I feel vindicated. The Schmidt Sting Pain Index lists the intensity of agony produced by different Hymenoptera – bees, wasps, ants and sawflies – and categorises them using everyday terms. The author, Justin O. Schmidt, is an entomologist at the Carl Hayden Bee Research Centre in Tucson, Arizona, and has the dubious pleasure of having been stung by the majority of the 78 species he has studied.

With the eloquence of a wine taster, he describes the following:

1.0 Sweat Bee: Light, ephemeral, almost fruity. A tiny spark has singed a single hair on your arm.

1.2 Fire Ant: Sharp, sudden, mildly alarming. Like walking across a shag carpet and reaching for the light switch.

1.8 Bullhorn Acacia Ant: A rare, piercing, elevated sort of pain. Someone has fired a staple into your cheek.

2.0 Bald-faced Hornet: Rich, hearty, slightly crunchy. Similar to getting your hand mashed in a revolving door.

2.0 Yellowjacket: Hot and smoky, almost irreverent. Imagine W. C. Fields extinguishing a cigar on your tongue.

2.0 Honey Bee and European Hornet: Like a matchhead that flips off and burns on your skin.

3.0 Red Harvester Ant: Bold and unrelenting. Somebody is using a drill to excavate your ingrown toenail.

3.0 Paper Wasp: Caustic and burning. Distinctly bitter aftertaste. Like spilling a beaker of hydrochloric acid on a paper cut.

4.0 Tarantula Hawk Wasp: Blinding, fierce, shockingly electric. A running hair drier has been dropped into your bubble bath.

4.0+ Bullet Ant: Pure, intense, brilliant pain. Like fire-walking over flaming charcoal with a 3-inch rusty nail in your heel.

Only on my return to the UK did I realise that I had undergone one of birding's great rites of passage, deserving of the ornithological world's Purple Heart for being wounded in the line of duty. But whenever I see David, Jonathan or Mark I still flush with embarrassment about the day I burst into tears because of a mere insect sting.

Desert Colours

Israel, 1997

The fresh-faced airport security officer looked to be straight out of school but had the uncompromising demeanour of an army veteran who had served on a brutal frontline. He studied me intently with icy eyes as if I was the world's most wanted terrorist. He was the walking embodiment of 'unfriendly': aloof, cold, frosty and inhospitable. By contrast, I was on a birding high – garrulous, happy, full of bonhomie. The blend was to prove toxic.

'What have you been doing in Israel?' The official asked with a sharpness that matched both his suit and the acerbic look he gave the moment I had first broken into a toothy smile, a tactic I thought best to support a passport photograph that was almost ten years old.

'Birdwatching,' I beamed.

'Bird. Watching.' He deliberately spaced the words as if he had never heard of anything so absurd.

'And where have you been?' His voice dropped an octave to emphasise his growing displeasure at my cheeriness.

'Oh, lots of places...'

He looked up with a snort and signalled for a colleague to join him. Gulp! I was to be grilled by clones. I expected the good cop bad cop treatment. I got a double serve of the latter.

'Where did you say you've been?' My original inquisitor asked.

It was straight bat time.

'Oh, just Eilat and the Neg—' Halfway through replying, I remembered parts of the Negev were home to some of Israel's most secretive and forbidden military establishments. I gave another gulp.

'Have you been to Jordan, Egypt or the West Bank?' the second security officer asked, his trained eyes staring intently, conducting their own lie detector test.

'No, no, no...' My voice must have sound like a castrato choirboy. They had cracked me. I was singing like a Canary (or should that be a Syrian Serin?). But their inquisition was far from finished.

'Open your case!' Officer One ordered, rolling back his shirt sleeves ready for action.

Out of the morass of birding paraphernalia and travelling detritus, he fished out my telescope then peered through from both ends like an antiques expert confronted with a weird collectible. The process was repeated with my binoculars before he homed in on my birding notebook; opening it delicately and pawing it like a key piece of evidence. For what seemed an age, he ran a finger over days of neatly jotted sightings as if he was twitcher supreme Lee Evans playing judge, jury and executioner on my records. I imagined him thinking: 'Grey Hypocolius – bloody stringer.'

Suddenly, he whispered something in Hebrew to his colleague, pointed at one of the pages of my notes and delved back into my travel holdall. This time the field guide came out.

'What's this bird?' He snapped.

My God, a bird quiz! His finger was perched on a picture of Tristram's Grackle.

'Tristram's Grackle.' I said with relief as if my very freedom depended on getting the question right.

'And this?' He was pointing at a Blue-cheeked Bee-eater. Trick question, I thought. I had missed them during the week-long trip.

'Blue-cheeked Bee-eater.' I responded smugly.

I got the slightest of nods, hardly Jeremy Paxman's *University Challenge* exuberance. I had two out of two, but now I was praying that he did not turn to the wheatears... or the gulls. Please not the gulls, I whispered to myself. I had spent so many hours being dragged around the rubbish tips of Bedfordshire by Gullmeister Martin Garner that I long thought the multitude of large, white-headed Larids should all be lumped as 'Sea Gull' (*Larus confuseus*). Instinctively, I shut my eyes and let my mind whir through the wing patterns of Heuglin's, Caspian and Armenian Gulls. I felt doomed.

My inquisitor's mind was whirring, too. His fingers fanned the pages like a casino dealer playing with a card deck. Go on then, wise guy, I mused. Go for the larks. You may think they're tough but I am ready for you. I had just been treated to a master class in lark identification by two of the finest birdwatchers in the world.

A week earlier, birdsong had woken me on my first chilly morning in Eilat, the sweet, thrush-like refrains bombarding my hotel bedroom from all directions. As morning alarms go, it was loud and efficient, but there was no snooze button. Once the deliberate phrases had created an irritating ear worm, I was up and whistling it to myself, excited by the thought that I was in a new country and there were new birds to see. Sunrise was still more than an hour away. I busied myself trying to find the culprit behind my wake-up call, picking my way through *Birds of the Middle East and North Africa*. I guessed Tristram's Grackle. I was wrong.

Within seconds of walking out of the hotel, I met my tormentor sitting on top of a date palm, singing the song still buzzing in my brain. Night had not yet become day, but there was enough light to get a good binocular view of the loud miscreant, a bland, brownish bird with a dark 'hood' – no wonder it was such a delinquent. A yellowish vent and white spectacles at least provided some field marks to hurriedly note down. I began scribbling a sketch as if confronted by a great rarity, but the same, fluty song echoing around the local park was a clue to the species's ubiquity. On plate 21, I finally married up my coarse sketch to the field guide's illustration. I had managed to miss Yellow-vented Bulbul (better known today as Spectacled Bulbul) during the weeks of 'cramming' for the trip, but that's bulbuls for you, so nondescript they should be called 'bore-buls'.

Across the road in Ofira Park, the fleeting shapes of birds darting in and out of the shrubbery and also parading on the manicured lawns suggested I would not be bored much longer. There may be a few purists who sneer at the idea of birding in town centre parks but there's nothing like the thrill-a-minute sensations of being in a new country and being drenched in a tidal wave of activity. Eilat's Ofira Park, or Shulamit Gardens, as it is often called, must be one of the best located pieces of urban green space anywhere in the world, especially when it comes to watching migration fallout. For the myriad nocturnal migrants on their last reserves of body fat after long flights up the Gulf of Aqaba, the postage stamp-sized piece of greenery is a glistening emerald in a sombre, brown desert. Birds are simply too exhausted to worry about inquisitive birdwatchers as they make emergency touchdowns to take on fuel and water. For birders, every step produces something new: Black-headed and Sykes's Wagtails parade across the lawns, joined by Water Pipits in rosy, spring finery. Bluethroats, their sapphire gorgets without the blemish of red or white spots (perhaps an indicator that they belong to one of the races from the Caucasus) prefer foraging in shade, although occasionally they emerge into the open so that the sun brings out the metallic sheen of their eponymous markings. Wrynecks disregard the camouflage protection provided by their bark-like plumages and work the freshly watered grass for insects. The rich terracotta hues of Cretzschmar's Bunting (difficult to pronounce but easy to admire) are accentuated by the irrigated greenness. Overhead, clouds of grey-rumped Rock Doves fill the skies on a mad, morning commute into Jordan, untroubled by their flight over the heavily guarded border. Before hunger pangs produce thoughts of breakfast, new shapes form in the clear skies – raptors are on the move.

Eilat's bird of prey migration has become the stuff of legend. Throughout the 90 days of spring more than a million birds pour overhead; various species seemingly allocated periods when they have domination of the skies. Steppe Buzzards monopolise in March, Levant Sparrowhawks through April and Honey Buzzards in May, but with them come a host of other powerful-winged migrants. Young Steppe Eagles with their distinctive covert patterns, and blonde adult Eastern Imperial Eagles provide that birding buzz when you pick them up in the scope and count off their various distinctive field marks. Short-toed Eagles and Booted Eagles are also in the mix, and birders prepared to put in the hours have come up with some of the most eagerly sought birds in the Western Palearctic, namely Bateleur, Verreaux's Eagle and Crested Honey Buzzard. Above Eilat in the Moon Valley Mountains, raptorphiles from across Europe gather to put their zoom eyepieces and identification knowledge to the test, earning respect from their peers as they identify, age and sex every tiny speck passing overhead. Sitting among these luminaries is humbling, especially when time and again they call out an eagle or hawk at an incredible distance, long before your own eyes have detected the merest hint of anything resembling a raptor shape. Each morning, for two or more hours, birds pour north, some at eye level, so close you can almost feel the brush of their primary feathers, others high and buoyant on the thermals created by the strong sun and stark desert geography. Even when the day's proceedings seem to have come to an end, the skies are never empty. No daylight hour during my stay in Eilat was devoid of birds of prey. Late in the afternoon, lone eagles and single buzzards still flapped wearily overhead, reinforcing a cardinal discipline I was taught on my first day in Israel: always look up. It is a principle that was to stand me in very good stead.

The desire to witness raptor migration in all its glory had burned away since I was a youngster, poring over maps that displayed migration routes with bottlenecks over Turkey's Bosphorous and Gibraltar. As Israel's place in these incredible journeys came to the fore and tensions with Arab neighbours diminished, the country became ever more popular as a destination for leading tour companies, with the likes of the late, great Peter Grant and bird artist supreme Killian Mullarney trail-blazing to desert soils made all the more fertile for birders by the work of one man – Hadoram Shirihai.

In the late winter of 1997 I met up with Hadoram in Tring, Hertfordshire, to conduct an interview for my weekly newspaper column. He had recently written the encyclopaedic *The Birds of Israel*, and we spoke at length about how he had learnt about the art of bird ringing on Fair Isle and had thrown himself into studying Eilat's astounding raptor migration. Hadoram Shirihai is 'something of a phenomenon' said the publisher's briefing notes, adding 'a modest need for sleep, a keen eye and a retentive memory are the qualities that have earned him this reputation.'

A few weeks later I was to witness his incredible skills for myself when I joined him and Killian's tour group as migration time was going into overdrive. As a tabloid journalist, particularly one with what might be perceived as an annoying habit of constantly asking inane questions, I sensed that my presence in such esteemed company may not have been warmly welcomed. One piece of luck was to change that.

That first morning in the park, an excursion to the Moon Valley Mountains and subsequent walks around Eilat's tapestry of habitats – date palms, salt pans, beach and desert scrub – created a non-stop procession of dawn-to-dusk memories that are still imprinted in my mind's eye as if they happened yesterday. There were vast sunrise flocks of Garganey coming ashore after spending a night roosting on the salty waters of the Gulf of Aqaba; the freshly arrived Eastern Olivaceous Warblers tail-bobbing in Ofira Park; lark flights in the pristine desert of the Arava Valley; marauding Barbary Falcons on the prowl for tired migrants; magnificent Hooded and Mourning Wheatears still at work in the heat of the day; waders bathed in the warm afternoon glow of early evening light; Lichtenstein's Sandgrouse taking fresh water onboard as soon as the skies darkened and then, in the cold still of the desert night, a Hume's Owl staring intently with tiger-like eyes the colour of fire.

One afternoon we had been tirelessly working an area of sewage pools on the trail of a diffident and not-so Clamorous Reed Warbler, when fatigue and the need for the kind of adrenalin fix that can only be produced by a new bird began taking hold. After an age staring at dank reed fronds, I remembered my newly learnt rule: always look up. Almost immediately, a mixed flock of chattering hirundines passed overhead, squabbling and playing tag on their flight north. Among the elongated streamers of the Barn Swallows and the House Martins' chiselled fork-tails, one shape stood alone. Size-wise, it seemed hardly bigger than a Sand Martin although its wings were more streamlined and its flight fluttery. Then, there was its square-tipped tail. My mind went into overdrive, searching deep in its repository of forgotten bird facts. 'Little Swift!' I screamed.

Everyone looked up as the bird did an elegant flypast, displaying its scimitar-shaped wings and a glistening white rump. As one of the best tour leaders in the business, Killian was always quick to heap praise on the finder of a good bird. Now I was getting his plaudits. I went the colour of a Sinai Rosefinch. Throughout his many visits to Israel, Killian had only seen Little Swift a few times. At last, I felt I was no longer an interloping cuckoo and I could take my place alongside the pukka birders on the tour. Killian had always been a charming, selfless tour leader, but now I sensed I had arrived in his eyes. I was birder first, a Fleet Street hack second.

Over subsequent days I was to learn a lot from Killian as he explained the finer points of identification in his lilting Irish tones. Whether it was creating the perfect field sketch with easy flicks of a pencil, or describing the calls of the various larks lurking among the rocky desert floor, his skill at explaining the most esoteric birding subjects matches his brilliant artwork. One day I remember watching Killian and Hadoram pondering the world of harrier identification with much animated gesturing of hands when a beautiful female Pallid Harrier glided across a kibbutz field. Later, they took time to explain the minutiae of one of birding's most esoteric areas so that the entire group had a better understanding of how to separate 'ringtail' Pallid from the very similar Montagu's.

Hadoram's place in Israeli ornithology was established long before he wrote his authoritative work on the country's birds. His reputation, however, goes well beyond his nation's birding community. I do not know if the following anecdote is true or not, but I was told it a few years ago and it places Hadoram not just in the Pantheon of all time birding greats but marks him out as a true institution. So it goes, two British birders on the trail of an elusive bird, say a Cream-coloured Courser or a Macqueen's Bustard, take a drive off the beaten track in the desert only to be confronted by the menacing shape of a Merkava tank. The turret opens and out pops the head of an Israeli officer who starts shouting at them in Hebrew. The two birders, eyes fixed on the tank's 120 mm, laser-guided gun, can only look on with absolute dread. One plucks up the courage and winds down the window to explain that they are only birdwatching.

With that, the Israeli soldier, in perfect English, warns them that they could have been shot.

'But we're trying to find a bird that Hadoram Shirihai has seen,' explains the driver.

'Ah, Hadoram,' the soldier muses. 'Okay then. Have a nice day.' Whether it is an urban myth or not, this story reinforces Hadoram's standing in Israel as well as across the wider, international birding community.

For all the excitement of a daily diet of new birds, the best was still to come. On our penultimate day we drove out of Eilat to look for one of the Western Palearctic's most eagerly sought-after species, Arabian Warbler, a hefty *Sylvia* not too dissimilar from Eastern Orphean Warbler but with an extremely limited range in the region – and a reputation for playing hard to find in dense acacia. To give ourselves a good chance we set off before sunrise, unaware of the events we were about to witness.

The following essay was runner up in the 2001 *BBC Wildlife* magazine travel writing competition and tells the story of the day colour came to the desert.

Colours, like water, are hard to find in Israel's unforgiving Negev Desert. Brown affronts the senses from all directions. Deep, dark caramel escarpments blend naturally with the soft coffee hues of the endless hammada. The few strands of wispy vegetation scattered among the rock-strewn floor are seared to a milky cocoa, encrypting the desert's masters of disguise: the scattering of larks, sandgrouse, wheatears and bustards that eke a living in this inhospitable land. Tan and fawn plumages, disrupted cunningly by delicate streaks and spotting, make perfect camouflage. A puff of dust or the ruffle of a wing may, momentarily, betray a bird's presence, but all too quickly it disappears, consumed by the heat-haze and the Negev's unique, tawny colour schemes. Then, for a few short weeks, it's spring. A verdant coating caresses the land. Acacias unfurl fresh green sprigs, saltbushes burst into life and ground-hugging plants blossom. The air is alive with birds as colourful as jewel-encrusted crowns: Bluethroats with iridescent turquoise gorgets, emerald Green Bee-eaters, Yellow Wagtails looking as if they have been dipped in gold and ruby-red Sinai Rosefinches. Birdwatchers follow. Few forces are stronger in nature than the hormone-driven will to mate. For countless millennia, long before Moses led his followers out of the Sinai, long before the first man hunted for gazelle with flints picked from the desert floor, birds have braved this arid land to reach their northern European breeding grounds. How fitting that the very route which brings millions of migratory birds to the Negev was sculpted by another of nature's powerful forces – the incredible energy deep inside the Earth that creates continents, mountains and valleys. The Great Rift Valley – forged 50 million years ago – is a 4,000-kilometre conduit for birds travelling from the Tanzanian savannah, across the Horn of Africa, along the Red Sea coastline, over the Gulf of Aqaba and finally up into the Israeli heartlands. For young songbirds, the Rift Valley acts as a handrail, guiding them ever northwards. Eagles and buzzards are also aided; the valley's steep escarpments, baked by the sun's incessant rays, produce rising thermal currents that allow graceful and, more importantly, effortless flight.

Since the Seventies, birdwatchers from across Europe have made springtime pilgrimages to the Holy Land to witness the migration spectacle. It begins in early March with the first vanguard squadrons of Steppe Eagles. Numbers build up and so does the variety of species: Eastern Imperial and Lesser Spotted Eagles, Black Kites, Steppe Buzzards, diminutive Levant Sparrowhawks and Honey Buzzards. By noon each day the skies over the coastal resort of Eilat are pitted with the distinctive, fingered wing-shapes of thousands of raptors circling and spiralling ever northwards on unseen air currents. Far below, warblers and chats take daytime refuge in the Negev's scattered cultivations and irrigated kibbutz fields. Many of these small passerines migrate by night, guided by the stars, and then take advantage of the new day's milky light to replenish their bodies by foraging in the scant vegetation for insects. Birdwatchers are active, too. It's a little after 6 a.m.: dawn's first gleaming has left the sky an eerie purple the colour of a Cadbury's chocolate wrapper, complementing the desert's cocoa tones. In the distance a Hoopoe Lark performs its strange display-flight, ascending on butterfly wings high into the sky before plummeting in a spiral, its melancholy song fading before it reaches the ground. Bar-tailed Larks provide the chorus, sounding like rusty pub signs swinging in the breeze. This is pristine desert, as yet spared the encroachment of Man with his irrigation channels and cash crops. But the moment is spoiled. Eyes adjusting to intensifying light pick out strange white shapes. Bags. Shopping bags. I am surrounded by high street detritus, a sea of white plastic shopping bags, gently fluttering in the softest of morning breezes. I investigate. A full-scale litter collection is impossible, but I make a token effort, advancing towards the nearest clump of ragged plastic. It moves. What was once a crumpled heap evolves into the graceful contours of a bird, a White Stork. Its head rises, exposing the dagger-shaped, crimson bill, and with a shudder, a pair of giant black and white wings spring from its body and flap frantically. The reaction is contagious. Other plastic bags mutate into storks.

Hundreds. Thousands. Tens of thousands. The air vibrates with wing-flapping; the first bird gains lift off. Then a second... Around me, the white plastic carpet has become a cloud, a cloud with an innate intelligence. Inexplicably, it forms into a twisting corkscrew, ever rising, ever increasing in volume as new birds join the mass. Below, I gaze upwards, awe-struck. Pied wings conspire with the Negev's unique geology and the desert sky to produce a kaleidoscope of subtle tones, pigments and shades before drifting to the north. Colour has come to the desert.

Back at airport security... I had got two questions right but Israeli airport security staff had not finished with my inquisition. Surely they no longer thought I was some kind of terrorist. Only a birder carries this much gear, I mused, looking at the various items the security officers had taken out of my holdall and lined up on an examination table. One officer whispered in the other's ear and he, in turn, looked at me with a devilish grin. They were about to play their trump card. More whispers followed before the first guard picked up my trusty, battle-worn Peterson guide to the *Birds of Britain and Europe*. I had brought it along more out of habit than as practical help. The nearest its geographical range came to Israel was Greece.

'And what is this?' The guard's finger alighted on the middle of three birds on Plate Six, the top of his nail obscuring its name. I took one look.

'White Stork,' I answered with a clenched fist as if I had just scored a cup final goal.

The guard almost smiled.

'Have a good flight,' he answered, handing back my passport.

International Rescue

Cyprus, 2005

On a scrub-covered hillside overlooking Ayia Napa's pulsating night lights death lurks in the bushes. Bird poachers are at work, scurrying through razor-sharp tangles of acacias, preparing to reap a cruel and barbaric harvest. The spoils are huge. Shadowy people pay small fortunes to sample the stomach-wrenching delights of a roasted songbird, bones and all. Gangsters pile tables with the carcasses of small, wild birds, only too ready to fight for their spoils, and fight dirty. Anyone standing in their way faces a chilling arsenal of stun guns and CS gas sprays.

Across the hillside, an undercover police team waits in the thick, gluey blackness, briefed and determined to end an outrage that shames their island. The first sounds of battle begin. Artificial birdsong fills the warm night air, the amplified warbles and twitters filtering into the dark to lure unsuspecting migrant birds from the skies and into trappers' clutches. A web of nets and sticks coated with thick glue await the warblers, robins, chats and shrikes heading south for the winter. Little do I realise that their fate is in my hands.

'Anyone cruel and sadistic enough to slaughter small birds is unlikely to flinch at using violence to avoid arrest.' Sergeant Kyriacos Elia's warning words still ring in the ears of his dozen-strong squad of officers staked out in the gloom.

'These guys are on drugs and will not hesitate to use violence. They have electric stun guns and also pepper sprays. One used a spray on me the other week,' the tough-looking, London-born policeman cautions.

I feel my stomach knot. Having been invited to watch the Sovereign Base Areas Police mount an operation against the ever-sophisticated gangs of bird trappers, I realise that the brave, dedicated policemen about to go on patrol are putting their lives at risk. The rewards are scandalous; the odds high; the bird-trappers ruthless. Yet there are collars to be felt, birds to be saved and equipment to seize. Sergeant Elia is also waiting to turn the tables on the young crooks, members of a notorious hoodlum gang fuelled by drugs and major players in one of Cyprus's most detested crimes. Disrupting an illegal poaching operation will be a major success, trapping a few trappers a bonus.

Under a moonless autumn sky and in total radio silence, we have driven to a vantage point with our 4x4 vehicle's lights blacked out. We crouch and wait. Suddenly, out of the darkness an off-road motorbike roars up. The trappers are coming. Chasing a suspect is not an option on treacherous limestone rocks where any careless footfall can break an ankle. To get an arrest, police have to catch the trappers at work. The stakeout continues. I wait patiently for a signal to move.

Ayia Napa is still in full swing as the first rays of sunlight emerge on the eastern horizon. We get our signal to move to the frontline. At the bottom of the hill the fearsome Cypriot police squad has converged, officers are gesticulating and talking excitedly.

'The trappers managed to get away,' admits Sergeant Elia, yet he does not seem disappointed. 'But they left behind their traps. It has been an expensive night for them.'

Trappers' nets, secretly imported from China at up to £80 each, dot the landscape. The police operation has cost the poachers dearly and now the race is on to locate the nets and release their terrified, exhausted quarry. It is time for me to play a part in the operation. In temperatures of more than 30 °C, a one-ounce Blackcap will dehydrate and perish quickly. Every net holds a handful of birds, each hopelessly ensnared by the fine mesh wrapped around their spindly legs. The birds look forlorn, terrified, a few heartbeats from death. My time to help has come.

No matter how much I would have loved to have taken on the scum who had set those heartless traps in hand-to-hand fighting, legal niceties and the fact that most of the thugs were half my age and a lot fitter than me meant that I had to stand behind the lines as the police operation went into gear with cautionary words of warning: do not move – it's dangerous. Standing alongside me was the Royal Society for the Protection of Birds' Grahame Madge who had arranged for us to witness the efforts being made to tackle a scourge that blights the name of Cyprus and its proud people.

Mediterranean islands have had a long tradition of hunting birds. Once, hungry people saw the seasonal flights as a supplement to protein-deficient diets but we are now in the 21st century: food is relatively cheap and migratory birds, already facing the perils of habitat destruction and the effects of climate change across their ranges, are deserving of protection. European laws are tough; their enforcers in the British controlled areas of Cyprus are uncompromising. Sadly, in too many back street tavernas or at traditional Cypriot family feasts, a pickled Blackcap is a prized and expensive delicacy. A single bird provides only a mouthful but since the trade was made illegal 30 years ago, connoisseurs of *ambelopoulia* – Greek for vine bird – pay handsomely for illicit indulgence. At £3 a bite there is a big incentive to risk some of Europe's harshest conservation penalties to plunder the sky of its most beautiful creatures. To compound the outrage, the traps are indiscriminate. Not only do birds targeted for the pot fall victim, but dazzling European Bee-eaters, noble Masked Shrikes, even the rare and endemic Cyprus Wheatear, are also indiscriminately captured in the nets or on gluey limesticks. Those birds still alive when trappers return have their throats slit and conservation workers are often brought to tears by the cruelty. One Scops Owl bit frantically through its own legs after becoming entangled in a net.

Such cruelty fuelled the zero tolerance stance of the SBA Police, the British law and enforcement agency charged with keeping order across almost 100 square miles of Cypriot countryside, a landscape sculpted by trappers. Millions of non-native acacias have been planted as cover for their nocturnal manoeuvres. Dotted between the vast green swathes of acacias are pomegranate and Syrian plum orchards; both trees are used for making the sticky limesticks to trap the birds.

At the SBA police headquarters in Dhekelia, divisional commander Jim Guy was in a no-nonsense mood to confront the organised racketeers when we met prior to the operation. The Glaswegian former chief superintendent cut his teeth in Strathclyde, dealing with more crime there in half a day than he faces in a year on Cyprus. There are still routine cases of theft, arson and football hooliganism, but bird trapping is a different challenge. In the station's operational briefing room, pictures of threatened Cypriot birds adorn the walls alongside strategic crime pattern maps. Even to a policeman with many years' service in one of the toughest beats in Europe, Glasgow city centre, bird trapping is particularly callous.

'It's a horrible way for anything to die. They trap everything under the sun, even protected birds,' he told me a few hours before his men went out into the darkness to deal a blow against the trappers.

In his Taggart-like accent, Mr Guy explained the riches on offer for those prepared to break the law.

'Over the past 15 years bird trapping has grown into a business where a successful trapper will make £30,000 in a season. A hunter can set up a mist net and catch up to 500 birds in an hour and will sell them wholesale for about £1.25 and they will be served up in a restaurant for around £3 each.

'Many Cypriots have the same attitude to bird-trapping as we would have to fishing back home and some fairly powerful people on the island share this view. At the peak of the trapping a few years back we estimate that up to 20 million birds a year were being caught. It is still a large-scale, big-money problem but we enforce the law very vigorously. We estimate that over the past five years, with the other agencies, we have saved up to 30 million birds.

'Our work is having an impact. We estimate a 90 per cent reduction in the number of trappers. Recently a deputation from one village said that where there used to be 300 hunters there were only 30 left. They asked if they could be allowed to hunt one hour a day. We do not compromise. We want to eradicate it completely. The hard core of poachers are becoming more sophisticated. They use lookouts when trapping and only put their nets up for a short time.'

With the trappers melting into the night, the precious nets are left billowing gently in the morning breeze, their movement interrupted by the frantic fluttering of bird wings. All eyes are suddenly on me. I have only minutes to inspect all the nets the police have discovered and release their unfortunate prisoners. The morning sun is rising fast, temperatures are increasing. My throat is dry and I can only imagine what effects dehydration is having on the birds left dangling in the sunlight. I have been awake for 24 hours but any feelings of tiredness are immediately forgotten once I begin extricating a young Blackcap that has become hopelessly ensnared in the fine, diaphanous netting. I am not a qualified BTO ringer but have handled enough birds to know the rudiments of net extraction. Untangling a freshly ensnared bird is one thing, trying to unravel a dying creature that has been left for hours to cocoon itself in thick layers of netting is a wholly new challenge.

Luckily, I do not have to worry about damaging the net – its value is only as evidence in any future prosecution. I use my nail to tear through the most awkward strands that have become entwined around the warbler's feet. The Blackcap's heart pounds in my hand. I fear that if I do not free it soon, the fright and tension will silence the bird's vital signs for good. One last, resolute piece of netting will not budge. I claw frantically until it pings. The Blackcap is free, my middle and index fingers still delicately placed either side of its shoulders. For a second, I look intently into its flickering eye, wondering whether it is strong enough to continue its journey over the sea and into Africa. I open my hand; it hesitates. Then, with a loud 'tchack' like two pebbles being hit together and a flap of its wings, it is gone. As a thank you, it has left a greasy dropping on my palm.

I have no time to admire my handiwork. Another net is bulging, this time with a larger, bulkier bird, its identity masked by the thick layers of black netting that obscure all of its markings. Already the hours of incarceration have taken their toll – the creature hangs limply like a ripe fruit waiting to be plucked. My fingers get to work as if I am playing a life-or-death game of Rubik's Cube. First, I claw in one direction, pulling away strands of netting around the bird's head; then I start the other way, attempting to release its feet. After a minute's fumbling I realise that I am nursing a shrike. I continue my precision work, always aware that a slip of my fingers will be fatal. The bird reacts. I feel its strength in my hands. It moves; wings and claws clambering for freedom. One final strand snaps with a reassuring twang. The shrike emerges, its metamorphosis from ensnared pupa into a splendid juvenile Masked Shrike complete. I have to overcome my momentary birder's desire to marvel at the intricate scalloped patterns of its scapulars and delicate tertial fringes. I am brought out of my momentary indulgence by a sharp pain. The shrike's hooked bill has got to work on my nail bed, attempting to butcher my cuticle as if it was impaling a beetle on a thorn. Pain forces me to relax my grip. Trappers bitten like this have one response: they tear the bird's beak off.

Sensing opportunity, the shrike opens its wings, frantically fluttering for liberty. I comply by raising my hand to form a launch pad. In an instant, it has gone. Not all birds are so lucky. As we work through the nets, I come across a Blackcap hanging close to the ground, upside-down and minus its head. A predator, perhaps a rat, had taken advantage of a quick meal, eating through the only part of the bird it could reach.

How many birds we saved that morning I do not know. Both Grahame and I worked frantically to clear the nets. Only the unfortunate Blackcap failed to continue on its travels. The police thanked us for our effort and we thanked them for theirs. Without the dedication of officers prepared to meet the scourge of trapping full in the face, putting life and limb at risk, Europe's migratory birds face a perilous time crossing the Island of Aphrodite.

Postscript

While our visit to Cyprus in the autumn of 2005 marked a successful period in cracking down on the bird trappers, there has since been a dramatic upsurge in the killing of migratory birds on the island. The findings of the most recent BirdLife Cyprus report make miserable reading. In 2010, a trained team of surveyors carried out its ninth annual monitoring programme and found things worse since monitoring began with an estimated death toll of up to 1.4 million birds within the Famagusta and Larnaca districts.

As I write this chapter, Martin Hellicar, BirdLife Cyprus campaigns manager, describes the slaughter as an 'ecological disaster' and says the trappers made hundreds of thousands of Euros selling Blackcaps and other birds.

The possible reasons for the resurgence are manifold and encompass international and internal politics as well as the downturn of the global economy. Major factors listed by BirdLife Cyprus include the wearing off of the 'EU effect', which was a vital catalyst for the first big enforcement push with the start of the new millennium. Cyprus is now a Member State rather than a candidate, and less wary of sanction from Brussels. Additionally, public demand for ambelopoulia remains high and the Cyprus government has never really got to grips with the restaurants serving the birds. The result is that the financial incentives for trapping remain massive. A tourism downturn and economic stagnation of recent years has only made trapping more attractive.

By Royal Appointment
The Falkland Islands, 2006

She sat blinking in the face of a South Atlantic gale: a giant, cuddly toy of a creature, nature's own answer to a Womble. All fluff and flab, her cuteness accentuated by black beady eyes, she had been designed to survive some of the harshest conditions on our planet. High in her remote cliff-top sanctuary, the bundle of soft, white down waited patiently, insulated against wind and rain, sleet and salt spray. Soon, she would be undergoing one of the natural world's great transformations from adorable chick to sleek flying machine – a powerful, Black-browed Albatross. Once her floppy wings had developed their powerful flight feathers, the albatross would begin her seven-year odyssey riding the waves. Only when she had matured into a beautiful porcelain-white adult would she return to the same craggy sanctuary on the remotest outcrop of the Falkland Islands to raise her own chick. As I gazed deeply into her black, limpid eyes I knew it would be a journey she was unlikely to survive.

For millions of years albatrosses have graced the high seas with their magnificent flights of fancy, careening over tempestuous waves on wings spanning up to 12 feet. Mariners throughout the ages were spellbound by the creature's mastery of the seas. To kill one, as Samuel Taylor Coleridge told in his epic poem *The Rime of the Ancient Mariner*, was a portent of catastrophe. For the 21 species of albatross, the superstition has proven prophetic.

Albatrosses have played an integral part in my life as a birder. I remember marvelling at a grainy black-and-white *Scottish Daily Express* picture of man in a flat cap offering food to a Black-browed on Lothian's Bass Rock back in the mid-Sixties, when I was still in short trousers and newly bitten by the bird bug. Little did I realise that 20 years later most probably the same bird – by then affectionately known to the twitching masses as 'Albert' – would help me get a job with Express Newspapers. One of Fleet Street's legendary editors, Brian Hitchen, was interviewing me for a job as an assistant news editor when, out of the blue, he asked if I had any hobbies. When I said 'birding', far from looking concerned that a would-be recruit to one of the toughest of jobs on a national newspaper spent his time watching feathered creatures, he simply asked what bird I wanted to see more than any other. I replied an albatross, and he urged me to explain myself, setting me off to regale Albert's tragic story of unrequited love as he tried year after year to woo the Gannets of Hermaness (by then Albert had relocated to Shetland). When I went to explain that poor Albert was forever trapped in the Northern Hemisphere, while his kinsfolk lived well south of the Equator, he punched the air with gusto and shook my hand with his vice-like grip.

'What a story. We must run it,' he enthused. 'When can you write it?'

I was hired.

I never did get to see Albert, though. He went missing that summer only to re-appear a couple of years later and although my newspaper published his fascinating story, it was written from a desk in London rather than in the face of a Shetland breeze. Although my dreams of seeing an albatross went unfulfilled, these birds were rarely out of my orbit, particularly when I was looking for material to put in my weekly columns. On one occasion I had the privilege to interview Sir David Attenborough and we spent a morning talking about his most memorable encounters with wildlife, touching on colourful birds of paradise, his meeting with Mountain Gorillas and sightings of mighty Blue Whales in the Pacific. For me, however, his most iconic television moment was the day he had his up close and personal encounter with a giant Wandering Albatross chick waiting for its parent to return to its grassy nest on South Georgia. Watching Sir David creep through the tussac grass to come eye-to-eye with the giant youngster waiting patiently for its parent to return from an epic journey thousands of miles across the South Atlantic Ocean with a crop filled with squid is the stuff of legend. I vowed to have my own 'albatross moment'.

Writing a weekly column for the *Daily Star* soon taught me that far from being merely a 'top of the wanted list' bird for ardent twitchers, there was also a terrible and disturbing story emerging about the plight of the albatross. Industrial-scale fishing was exacting a heavy toll on these long-lived but slow to reproduce birds, and I soon learned a dreadful statistic. Besides having the longest wing span of any bird, living longer than 60 years and being able to circumnavigate the planet on long oceanic flights, there was one fact that cast an appalling shadow over these beautiful birds:

every five minutes an albatross was doomed to a dreadful death by the recklessness of the fishing fleets sucking the seas dry. One important international figure highlighting this tragedy was HRH the Prince of Wales who had taken the albatross under his royal wing and was only too willing to champion its cause.

In March 2005, the appalling losses of albatrosses compelled Prince Charles to deliver a call to arms to preserve them for future generations. His words made a powerful piece for my *Sunday Express* column:

Like many other one-time mariners, I have a very special affection for the albatross. I remember so well, while serving in the Royal Navy, standing on the deck of a fast-moving ship in one of the southern oceans, watching an albatross maintaining perfect position alongside for hour after hour, and apparently day after day. It is a sight I will never forget. I find it hard – no, impossible – to accept that these birds might one day be lost forever. Yet that does now seem to be a real possibility unless we can make a sufficient fuss to prevent it. In 1996, three of the 21 species of albatross were listed as threatened. Four years later, when I sat down to write an article expressing my concerns about the decline of these magnificent birds, the total threatened species had risen to 16. Another five years on and 19 of the 21 species of albatross are now under threat of extinction with some species now numbering under 100 individuals. The albatross family is now the biggest single bird family with every one of its members under threat.

'I have always felt that if their wanderings should cease through man's insensitive hand and that magical moment of a swallow's first arrival or an albatross's return disrupted forever, then it would be as if one's heart had been torn out. If this was to happen – and we are rapidly approaching the very real possibility with all 21 species of albatross – then we would sacrifice any claim whatsoever to call ourselves civilized beings. We will have violated something sacred in the inner workings of nature, and our descendants will pay dearly for the consequences of this and other acts of short-term folly.'

A few weeks later, I was standing in line awaiting an introduction to Prince Charles to talk about his efforts to stem the tide of albatross destruction. The occasion was a Royal Society for the Protection of Birds gala dinner where the Prince would be making a keynote speech to underline his message. Struggling to get an expanding waist into a mysteriously shrunken dinner suit, I never thought for a moment that I would get an opportunity to speak to Charles about his love for these sublime flying machines, but soon after his arrival at the London venue for the dinner, a Clarence House aide approached me and said that the Prince would like to thank me personally for what I had written about his campaigning.

Seconds later, I was in a line of RSPB officials, awaiting my audience and trying to remember the protocols of using 'Your Royal Highness' and then 'Sir' at the appropriate moments and remembering only to answer questions and not ask them. Suddenly, Charles was standing in front of me with a broad smile, not as tall as I imagined, but with the firmest and friendliest of handshakes, delivered with real, hefty farmer's hands. His chunky fingers were twice the size of mine. I went rubber mouthed, mumbling my words like a schoolboy asked to address class assembly when he thanked me for the articles I had written. I sensed he was aware of my nervousness and so he put me on firmer ground – talking about albatrosses. He asked if I had ever seen an albatross and when I answered 'no, Sir,' he urged me to get my editor to send me to New Zealand so I could visit Taiaroa Head, the only mainland breeding ground for the awesome Northern Royal Albatross. The sincere and heartfelt emotion he obviously held for these birds was patent, and his every word about them not only exuded admiration but also fears for their very survival. I could have stood there chatting for hours but royal duties meant there were other hands to shake. Eleven months later, the prince's suggestion came true. I was sitting on an RAF flight to Port Stanley with my good friend and RSPB colleague Grahame Madge. We were off to do our bit to save the albatross.

Grahame is a genial and deeply committed mainstay of the RSPB's media team. Colleagues in the press liken him to a Scotland Yard detective due to his burly frame and tenacious eagerness to get things done, and he has become known affectionately as 'Detective Sergeant' Madge because he always gets his man or, in newspaper terms, he always makes sure journalists in his care get their story. The 'DS' has an incredible knowledge of conservation issues and is also an excellent photographer. He is a very keen birder, too. As soon as we touched down on Ascension Island for a refuel and leg-stretch halfway through our 20-hour flight, we were busy scanning the skyline for arguably the rarest bird on the British List – Ascension Frigatebird, added courtesy of a 1953 record of a moribund female found on Tiree. Looking out over the desolate volcanic terrain, three 'Man o' War Birds' were floating piratically along the coastline on distinctive backward-angled wings. The first tick of the trip, but building a life list was very much a secondary issue – we had an international scandal to expose.

With us on the flight were veteran broadcaster John Craven and a film crew from the BBC's *Countryfile* programme. They were making a special about life on the Falklands archipelago which would feature a section on the plight of the albatross. John has always been something of a hero of mine. His classic children's programme *John Craven's Newsround* had first aired in the early Seventies at a time I was mulling over career choices, and his unique brand of no-nonsense broadcasting, which informed youngsters without patronising them, was hugely instrumental in my decision to take up journalism. His people skills are brilliant and while Grahame and I were busy trying to get views of the frigatebirds, John was chatting with servicemen wanting to pose for photographs and get his autograph. John duly obliged with big smiles and handshakes before we climbed aboard the 747 for the next leg of the journey. Eight hours later we were descending through thick South Atlantic cloud with a welcome party of two RAF Tornados on our wings, a spectacular way of letting the world know that the Falklands are as much a part of Britain as Falmouth or Falkirk and that the names inscribed on the memorial to the fallen of the 1982 war that stands proudly on the Port Stanley seafront will never be forgotten.

Waking early the next morning it felt like I had never left Britain. After a full English breakfast at my digs I took a walk in the dawn half-light along Port Stanley's main high street – the homely sounding Ross Road – contemplating how I had travelled halfway around the world to find myself in the Southern Hemisphere's equivalent of the Isles of Scilly. Only those who have experienced the time-lapse atmosphere of St Mary's, Tresco or St Agnes, with the friendly, almost naive, outlook on life, will understand how you feel that you have been plucked from the 21st century and dropped back to the more conservative times of the Fifties. Little traffic, litter free gutters, blank walls with no hint of graffiti and neatly laid out Victorian-style, brick villas with freshly painted picket fences and immaculate gardens were a reminder of my childhood on a London overspill estate in deepest Bedfordshire. A look at my GPS showed that I was at virtually the same parallel south as I was brought up in the northern hemisphere – 51° 41' 31'. Only when I looked out across Port Stanley harbour was there a hint that I was in foreign parts: a Magellanic Penguin, all black-and-white stripes as if it had been slipped into a Newcastle United shirt, was swimming merrily 100 metres off shore. This was my first wild penguin. Feeding time at Whipsnade Zoo is hardly comparable to focusing on your own truly wild bird bobbing on the sea like a fattened-up Razorbill. I zoomed in with my scope to savour the moment only to lose sight as an ugly grey mass swept past. A Stinker! Stinker is the pejorative nickname given to the Southern Giant Petrel by Falkland Islanders because of its unsavoury eating habits, with sewage and long-dead offal being preferred dining options. An ability to digest just about any organic matter means that they do a good job of keeping the Port Stanley shoreline as pristine as its roads. Luckily, the bird was downwind as it glided past, scraggy-faced and unkempt, on wings as stiff as a shearwater and long enough to match those of an albatross. I prayed for the Black-browed to be more charismatic.

There was time for a full day's birding around the capital before we headed off on the next leg of the mission and so Grahame and I decided to take a bumpy, off-road excursion down to Bluff Cove, scene of the infamous Argentine attacks on RFA *Sir Galahad*. The cove has become a popular attraction thanks to its star performers the Gentoo Penguins. They waddle around the sweeping picture postcard beach on feet that look like bright orange flip-flops, grumbling out loud as if they own the place and do not like being peered at and photographed by day-trippers hot off a docked cruise liner. As a birder I took the moral high ground, feeling a little more entitled to watch the penguins' zany comedy routines, with them scuttling along like miniature Charlie Chaplins, wings akimbo. Who said you should never anthropomorphise wildlife, especially when it makes you laugh?

Among the thousand or so Gentoos stood a single young King Penguin, head and shoulders taller and with the first hint of its distinct orange breast markings. At the far end of the beach, a 'peep', caught my eye. The telescope's zoom was cranked up to 60x magnification but still the tiny wader remained a mystery until it turned side-on and its attenuated carriage became visible. Long wings extending way beyond the tail marked it out as a White-rumped Sandpiper, a small Calidrid busy feeding up prior to its 9,000-mile flight north to feed on the Arctic tundra.

As one may expect on such a remote archipelago, the birding was quality rather than quantity. During our short stay in Port Stanley, Grahame and I managed to see several Falkland Steamer Ducks, flightless eider-like birds that made heavy work crossing the harbour on stubby wings flailing like old Mississippi paddle boats. Upland Geese were everywhere and arguably the world's most beautiful Larid, Dolphin Gull, a real dandy of a bird with its Confederate Army-grey tones accentuated by the vermilion brilliance of its bill and legs, was an enjoyable find.

Passerines, meanwhile, were in particularly short supply and my notebook had to make do with only the rather bland Falkland Thrush (a washed out Blackbird, if truth be told), Correndera Pipit, the islands' equivalent of our Meadow Pipit, Long-tailed Meadowlark, Black-chinned Siskin and White-bridled Finch. Of course, there were introduced House Sparrows, but what would you expect in a city where the Governor's official car is a black London Cab, fish and chips is one of the favourite dishes and the pubs serve up English bitter? Of course, if our schedule had allowed, I am sure we could have gone exploring in the 'camp', Falklands' slang for the vast, bleak hinterland comprising thick, coarse vegetation, millions of sheep and, unfortunately, unexploded mines left over from the brief Argentine occupation. Time, however, was at a premium: we had a rendezvous to keep with a rather special bird.

As we took off on a cool, clear March morning from Port Stanley Airport and swept out over the untamed wilderness, one wondered why the Argentine junta was prepared to sacrifice so many lives to put the islands under its flag. The fact that the total landmass equates to an area the size of Northern Ireland but supports a population of only 3,000 might tell you something about the hardships and tough living conditions Falkland Islanders face on a daily basis. That said, they are a special breed: resilient, hospitable and proud to be British. Defending their sovereignty was most probably Margaret Thatcher's greatest achievement. The flight west took us over two of the conflict's key battlegrounds, Pebble Island, where the SAS destroyed an Argentine landing strip, and also San Carlos Water – so-called Bomb Alley – where the main amphibious invasion began. Our own journey was one filled with poignancy, but seeing the inhospitable ground where guys of my generation were killed and maimed fighting so far from home left me admiring the bravery of our servicemen and questioning my own inner strengths.

In less than an hour we were over one of the most westerly parts of the archipelago, Carcass Island, named after HMS *Carcass*, which first charted it in 1766. There to meet us on the grassy runway was its present owner Rob McGill, who welcomed us like long lost relatives. Rob has turned his farmstead into a popular stopover for Falkland Island tourists, particularly those wanting to watch wildlife. The absence of cats and rats on the island means that species such as the endemic Cobb's Wren flourish. There was little time to birdwatch, though. Apart from marvelling at the 'Johnny Rooks' – the local name for the Striated Caracara, one of the world's rarest birds of prey – loafing around Rob's garden, there were only a few moments to have some refreshments before we boarded the small fishing boat waiting to take us on the next stage of our quest.

The early morning greyness had long cleared and the sea and sky were bathed in shades of blue as the boat chugged away from Rob's jetty towards the deep waters of the Patagonian Sea. Looking back at Carcass Island with its sweep of gorse and rolling grassland, I was reminded of the bleak, austere beauty of St Agnes's Wingletang Down. Only the sight of a Rock Shag, resplendent in black-and-white garb and with brilliant red facial markings, was a clue to our true location deep in the Southern Hemisphere. Within ten minutes of moving into clear water came another reminder.

There is a wonderful feeling when things in your life click, when that last jigsaw piece fits snugly into the gap, when the person you have been dying to hear from picks up the phone, or when a garage appears on the horizon the moment your fuel gauge hits the empty mark. That's how I felt when looking out to sea and the colours, shape and charisma of a large black-and-white bird morphed into .... an albatross, my first albatross!

Holy Grail birds have the power to make grown men cry. I must admit I claimed to have something in my eye when I saw my first Wallcreeper. My first California Condor had me using the same excuse, but my first Black-browed Albatross? As it glided by, individual flight feathers adjusting to the slightest zephyr, I almost felt a sense of justice. Having travelled so far, written so much about their plight, I did not feel like I was witnessing a new bird in all its glory but rather that I was experiencing the coming together of two old friends: one a majestic master of the oceans, the other a jobbing hack who knew the seas would be all the less for their disappearance.

Soon albatross moments were coming thick and fast. The swell was being dissected by their tapering wings and inquisitive individuals were landing alongside the boat to inspect us with their black-shadowed eyes. Looking round at John Craven and his film crew busy at work and Grahame clicking his camera at full speed, the sense of awe being created by the occasion was palpable. Could the albatross astonish us any further? I doubted it.

After an hour or so out at sea, the boat turned and began heading towards another of the islands, this time West Point, one of the few areas of the entire archipelago where Black-browed Albatrosses come together to form compact nesting colonies on top of towering cliffs. To get there involved 'yomping' – a word made famous by the Falklands conflict – through strength-sapping tussac grass that towered above head height and conspired to trip me every step, but soon the air was filled with the garrulous sounds and fishy smells of a seabird city. Black-and-white shapes began appearing amid the grassy fronds; muddy nests like giant eggcups were decorated with fat, downy chicks. The moaning and groaning echoing across the hillside reached a crescendo. We had arrived.

Sitting down at a safe distance from a nest, I looked deep into the young albatross's eyes and listened intently as our guide, Grant Munro, the director of Falklands Conservation, lamented their story with tones of despair. Scottish-born Grant, a forester by profession, looked across at the chick wistfully as he spoke about its long-term fate.

'Albatrosses are remarkably tame birds, and if you sit quietly you can watch them as they await their parents' return,' he whispered. 'The chicks remain on the nest so they do not get lost before the adults return with food, often after spending up to several days at sea.'

Grant then turned to the conservation issue. 'Here, in the colonies, the birds are doing well. They have a successful breeding rate. The problems are at sea. We conduct a count every five years around the islands and that shows that the population is around 400,000 pairs but declining at the rate of around 15 per cent every decade. This equates to a breeding pair being lost every hour, which is very worrying. They are a long-lived species and do not have a high reproductive rate, so even a two per cent decline in the adult population can lead to a reduction which is difficult to recover from.'

The story I subsequently filed for the *Sunday Express* detailed how albatrosses were doomed to dreadful deaths by the recklessness of fishing fleets sucking the seas dry. Succulent squid for the restaurant tables of the Spanish Costas and Patagonian tooth-fish to delight expensive American palates had seen the bountiful waters patrolled by highly sophisticated fishing vessels from Brazil, Uruguay and Argentina equipped with trawls and lines lethal to any passing seabird. A three-inch hook baited with a piece of rotting fish was equally attractive to an unsuspecting albatross and yet millions of these floating death sentences were being cast into the seas by fishing boats whose 'long lines' stretch out 80 miles across the ocean. What seemed easy food for the bird all too quickly became its last meal. Before the hook sank, it floated menacingly on the swell for a few moments, enough time for a passing bird to grab the bait and find itself cruelly ensnared by the sharp barbs tearing into its throat. As the hook submerged, the bird drowned, slowly.

It was a story played out 100,000 times every year and saw 19 of the 21 species of albatross heading towards extinction. But there was hope. By fishing at night, fitting boats with bird-scaring devices, weighting lines and using thawed bait which sinks more quickly, the instances of albatross deaths were falling. While the Falklands territorial waters were witnessing successful mitigation measures, there were still other threats across the vast South Atlantic. Pirate fishing trawlers left albatrosses with smashed and damaged wings. Birds, drawn to the boats by the fish guts and offal being discarded over the side, stood no chance as the heavy metal flexes used to haul nets crashed down on their frail bodies. More sickening were the reports of albatrosses being deliberately caught by ravenous sailors on unregistered boats from the Far East. Conditions aboard were so appalling for the crews, paid a pittance and handed only survival rations of rice, that an albatross provided welcome protein during a year at sea.

Five years on, and the plight of the albatross has improved – slightly. Our visit to the Falkland Islands in 2006 coincided with the advent of the Albatross Task Force, a collaborative effort between the RSPB and BirdLife International which saw a team of dedicated instructors travelling to the bycatch hotspots in South America and southern Africa demonstrating mitigating techniques to reduce the horrendous number of bird deaths. The results have been impressive. For every 100 albatrosses being killed in fisheries in South African waters in 2006, 85 are now being saved. There have also been optimistic results in South America. In the south of Chile, the incidental capture of seabirds was reduced from over 1,500 birds in one year to zero through the adoption of modified fishing gear, while in Argentina the use of mitigation in trawl fishery has also shown that it is possible to reduce seabird mortality to close to zero. In Brazil, the voluntary adoption of simple bird-scaring lines has helped to reduce incidental capture of seabirds by 56 per cent. Albatrosses are still in peril. They still need the support and help of conservation organisations. But looking at the photograph of me coming face to face with that young Black-browed chick blinking in the wind, I can now hope that she has survived the perils of her early life and is still gracing the oceans in all her majesty.

Other Birding Titles by New Holland

Advanced Bird ID Handbook
Nils van Duivendijk
Award-winning guide covering the key
features of all the Western Palearctic's
1,350 species and subspecies.
£24.99 ISBN 978 1 78009 022 1

Atlas of Rare Birds
Dominic Couzens
Amazing tales of 50 of the world's rarest
birds, illustrated with a series of stunning
photographs and colour maps.
£24.99 ISBN 978 1 84773 535 5

Birds of Africa South of the Sahara
Ian Sinclair and Peter Ryan
More than 2,000 species covered in full
colour. The most comprehensive field
guide to the continent's birds.
£29.99 ISBN 978 1 86872 857 2

Birds of Indian Ocean Islands
Ian Sinclair and Olivier Langran
The first comprehensive field guide to
the birds of Madagascar, Seychelles and
Mauritius. Covers 359 species in colour.
£17.99 ISBN 978 1 86872 956 2

Chris Packham's Back Garden
Nature Reserve
Chris Packham. Explains the best ways
to attract wildlife into your garden, and
to encourage it to stay there.
£12.99 ISBN 978 1 84773 698 7

Colouring Birds
Sally MacLarty
Ideal gift to help develop a child's
interest in birds. Features 40 species.
£2.99 ISBN 978 184773 526 3

Common Garden Bird Calls
Hannu Jännes and Owen Roberts
Invaluable book and CD featuring the
songs and calls of 60 species, each
illustrated with photos and maps.
£6.99 ISBN 978 1 84773 517 1

Creative Bird Photography
Bill Coster
Illustrated with the author's inspirational
images. An indispensable guide to all
aspects of the subject.
£19.99 ISBN 978 1 84773 509 6

A Field Guide to the Birds of Borneo
Susan Myers
Features more than 630 species. The
only comprehensive and accurate field
guide to the varied avifauna of Brunei,
Sabah, Sarawak and Kalimantan.
£24.99 ISBN 978 184773 346 7

A Field Guide to the
Birds of South-East Asia
Craig Robson
New flexi-cover edition of the only
comprehensive field guide to this
biodiverse region. Fully updated,
illustrated in colour and covering all
1,300 species recorded.
£24.99 ISBN 978 184773

The Garden Bird Year
Roy Beddard
Gives both birdwatchers and gardeners
insights into how to attract resident and
migrant birds to the garden, and how to
manage this precious space as a vital
resource for wildlife.
£9.99 ISBN 978 184773 503 4

The History of Ornithology
Valerie Chansigaud
The story of more than two millennia of the study of birds. Richly illustrated with numerous artworks and photos and a detailed timeline of events.
£17.99 ISBN 978 1 84773 433 4

Kingfisher
David Chandler and Ian Llewellyn
Engaging and beautifully illustrated monograph of one of Britain's best-loved birds. Also available: *Barn Owl*.
£12.99 ISBN 978 1 84773 524 9

The Naturalized Animals of Britain and Ireland
Christopher Lever
Authoritative, readable account of how alien birds and animals were introduced and naturalized, their status and impact.
£35.00 ISBN 978 1 84773 454 9

New Holland Concise Bird Guide
An ideal first field guide to British birds. Covers more than 250 species in colour. Comes in a durable plastic wallet and includes a fold-out ID sheet.
£4.99 ISBN 978 1 84773 601 7
Also available in the Concise Guides series: *Butterflies and Moths, Garden Wildlife, Insects, Mushrooms, Seashore Wildlife, Trees* and *Wild Flowers*.

New Holland European Bird Guide
Peter H Barthel
The only truly pocket-sized comprehensive field guide to all the birds of Britain and Europe. Features 1,700 artworks of 500 species.
£10.99 ISBN 978 1 84773 110 4

SASOL Birds of Southern Africa
Ian Sinclair, Phil Hockey and Warwick Tarboton
The world's leading guide to southern Africa's 950 bird species. Each is illustrated in full colour.
£19.99 ISBN 978 1 86872 721 6

The Slater Field Guide to Australian Birds
Peter Slater, Pat Slater and Raoul Slater.
Fully updated edition of the comprehensive field guide. Features more than 750 species over 150 plates.
£14.99 ISBN 978 1 87706 963 5

Tales of a Tabloid Twitcher
Stuart Winter
The key birding events and personalities, scandal and gossip of the past 20 years through the eyes of a birding journalist. A 'must-read' book for birders.
£7.99 ISBN 978 1 84773 693 2

Top Birding Sites of Europe
Dominic Couzens
An inspiration for the traveling birder. Brings together a selection of the best places to go birding on the continent.
£22.99 ISBN 978 1 84773 767 0

The Urban Birder
David Lindo
Even the most unpromising cityscapes can be great for birds. Includes tales of run-ins with gun-toting youths and migration-watching from skyscrapers.
£9.99 ISBN 978 1 84773 950 6

See www.newhollandpublishers.com for further details and special offers